Snake

D1598859

Animal
Series editor: Jonathan Burt

Already published

Crow
Boria Sax

Ant
Charlotte Sleigh

Tortoise
Peter Young

Dog
Susan McHugh

Cockroach
Marion Copeland

Oyster
Rebecca Stott

Forthcoming

Rat
Jonathan Burt

Tiger
Susie Green

Parrot
Paul Carter

Fox
Martin Wallen

Snake
Drake Stutesman

Crocodile
Richard Freeman

Whale
Joe Roman

Cat
Katharine M. Rogers

Falcon
Helen Macdonald

Spider
Katja and Sergiusz Michalski

Bee
Claire Preston

Duck
Victoria de Rijke

Hare
Simon Carnell

Peacock
Christine Jackson

Moose
Kevin Jackson

Salmon
Peter Coates

Fly
Steven Connor

Wolf
Garry Marvin

Snake

Drake Stutesman

REAKTION BOOKS

To the beautiful S-*line and* F

Published by

REAKTION BOOKS LTD
79 Farringdon Road
London EC1M 3JU, UK
www.reaktionbooks.co.uk

First published 2005
Copyright © Drake Stutesman 2005

Printed and bound in China by C&C Offset Printing Co., Ltd

British Library Cataloguing in Publication Data

Stutesman, Drake
    Snake. – (Animal)
    1. Snakes 2. Animals and civilization
    I. Title
    597.9'6

ISBN 1 86189 239 X

Contents

Introduction

Sssssssssssssssssssss.

Do you hear a snake's hiss? If so, it's likely that a sudden involuntary feeling rushes you because everyone has an opinion about snakes. Emily Dickinson may have admitted something for all when, in her poem about a harmless garter snake, she says:

> But never met this fellow,
> Attended or alone,
> Without a tighter breathing,
> And zero at the bone.

Compare that to a young pet owner's enthusiastic 'My snake makes me happy' or the words of a contemporary Appalachian snake handler on the experience of holding one in church, 'it's full of joy. I feel like I'm walking in another world.'[1]

The snake is very much alive in today's cultures. Soothe yourself with a Chinese rheumatic snake remedy, spice your virility with a swig of snake's blood or boost your immune system with a snake's gall bladder. Show off a fanged serpent tattoo. Walk through the annual Texas Rattlesnake Roundup and see thousands of trapped rattlers killed and turned into souvenirs. Visit India's Cobra Festival, in Jodhpur, the *Naag Panchami,* where,

A schoolgirl with pet snakes, 1927.

for three days, handlers believe cobra venom has no effect. Listen to Australian Aboriginal warnings of languid pools guarded by giant water snakes. See women dancing with boa constrictors or pythons on the Internet or television or in clubs in Berlin, Manila and Las Vegas. Go to an American Holiness Church of Signs Following and watch people praying with live copperheads in their hands, attend the Festival of Snakes in Italy where snakes are paraded in the name of Christ or watch Hopi priests hold rattlesnakes between their teeth and dance in a day-long rain ceremony.

These are all contemporary events, each with ancient roots, some obvious, some obscured. It's strange that snakes mean so much yet it's easy to see why. They are exotic: their patterns are

Two *serpari* (snake-charmers) celebrate San Domenico's Day in Cocullo, Italy.

beautiful, their movement sexual, their shape muscular and primitive, their dexterity awesome, their toxicity oddly tantalizing. Their colours range from flaming reds, oranges and yellows to vibrant greens, stark whites and muddy browns interspersed with black. Their markings are mesmerizing watery-shaped geometries in sharply coloured patterns of diamonds, bands, stripes, gradations and dots. The snake is so deep in the human subconscious, it is the world's most symbolized animal and, from the Ice Age to the present, can be found in every walk of human life. In psychology and art, the snake is erotic. In fairy stories and epics, it's supernatural. In religion, it's moral. In cinema, it's monstrous. In folk tales, it's odd. In the military, it's magic. In clothing, it's exciting. In cuisine, it's provocative. This animal is still assigned a status found in names, tattoos, emblems, tales, mementos and cures. Equally, it is viewed with such fright that it endures intense persecution and, unlike other hunted animals, rarely enjoys protected rights.

The eternal snake arabesque.

Snakes evoke extremes of fear or admiration even among people who have never seen a real one. Their sinuous glide and dazzling patterns are wildly attractive, but their venomous fangs, surreptitious slither and unbreakable squeeze terrify. Why does the snake fascinate so? There are many reasons, both literal and psychological. As an animal, it is an evolutionary success. Ingeniously adaptable and enviably efficient, the snake could be said to be in tune with all the world's elements. Its temperature is that of the climate. It moves with equal ease on liquid or solid surfaces. It inhabits every kind of terrain – river, ocean, desert, forest, jungle, mountain – living in branches, holes, rocks, sand and water. It coils with elegant agility around any shape. It can be smaller than a finger or as big as a tree. The tiniest can poison in seconds and the largest squeeze a cow to death or swallow a pig whole. Most are harmless and helpful, controlling populations of rodents, insects and other pests. Some are lethal, equipped with venom able to kill in under an hour and containing degenerative properties that corrupt flesh in ways horrifying to see.

The snake's primordial system, functioning for over one hundred million years, is a marvel of genetic engineering. The snake smells with its tongue and hears with its flesh. It sees through a lidless eye, covered by a transparent scale, and its retina acts as a zoom lens. It propels itself by a locomotion of rippling muscles. It sheds its skin. It breaks off its tail. It has one lung. It breathes under sand. It has infrared radar. Its mouth unhinges to surround a body many times its size. Its digestion can take months. It copulates for days with one snake or fifty at once. It lays eggs, gives birth live or self-clones. Its penis and its clitoris are forked. Its gender when in the womb is determined by heat. It mimics death if afraid or induces spontaneous bleeding.

With all these qualities, it's easy to see why no other creature has inspired such contradictory emotions or such diverse symbolism. Virtually as long as humans have walked the earth, snakes have been worshipped, reviled, prized, totemized, tortured and collected. They have been given meanings ranging from resurrection, wisdom and divine female omniscience to world destruction, duplicity and male castration anxiety since humanity began to allegorize the natural world. Findlay Russell, a foremost expert on snakes and venoms, makes an interesting argument that venom and its terrors are at the root of the venerations and hatreds of snakes.[2] Certainly, venom makes the snake prominent but the human's mysterious infatuation with the snake encompasses more.

The lore is impressive. The snake has always had and continues to have cult dimensions spread across regions, countries, religions and millennia. It once was viewed as omnipotent. The subsequent meanings it has been assigned range from progenitor in creation myths and destroyer in Armageddon stories to the stuff of tall tales from folklore to Freud. In the East, it is virtually interchangeable with the dragon, the principle of change and regeneration; Asian snakes can be negative but are often good medicine, good food, good fortune and good sex. In the West, snakes are villains or saints, the defeated or the invincible, healers or monsters, even penises or vaginas. Added to the many emblems, the multiple interpretations of their meanings make the snake a nest of questions.

But vestiges of its first great broad strokes can still be found, though are often buried. The snake, however portrayed, maligned or appropriated over history, seems to be the symbol most quintessentially suited to the human imagination. It is global, weirdly consistent, and never less than cosmically themed, be it as medicine, concept or threat. Time is the snake's central motif. It is seen as infinite continuity, the action of process, the becoming of conception, the embodiment of immortality, the universal substance, and the current in artistic energy. It begins in the Palaeolithic era as a fertility or water source, becomes a prehistoric creator of the world and spreads out, over millen-

Kitagawa Utamaro, coloured wood-block print of a snake, from an album of *c.* 1788.

nia, into lavish philosophies regarding the nature of things. In Asia and Africa the snake by and large retains its ancient flavour but, by late antiquity, the Western snake increasingly loses its supremacy and decays into arcane or evil meanings. This transition continues into the twenty-first century. Nevertheless, cursory study shows that these connotations are ambivalent. Despite the slander, the snake never seems totally to shed its original cosmic power. Even today, archaic snake symbolism structures some of the most creative ideas in science and art.

There are many versions of serpent myths and they are intricate and seemingly contradictory. It is hard for modern readers to understand these contradictions; they are the result of an ancient philosophical understanding of the integration of

An uroboros emblem from George Wither's *Collection of Emblemes, Ancient and Modern* (1635), 'ends in its beginning'.

opposites as well as centuries of change. The details diversify but the themes remain, as if the old reverence for the snake cannot be truly dissolved. Permanent threads run through all ophidiophobia and ophidiodolatry. A few stand out as beautifully durable.

Two serpent symbols have remained constant as sublime expressions of the creative mind's ability to render abstract thought. They still evoke the same meaning as they did 20,000 years ago. They are the 'uroboros' and the 'serpentine line'. Both are graphically simple, both philosophically complex. The uroboros, first imagined in prehistoric times, depicts a snake rolled into a circle biting its own tail and demonstrates the concept of eternity. The serpentine line or the *S*-shape, taken from the snake's curling arabesque, also originates in prehistoric consciousness. It unrolls and extends the eternal line to demonstrate the concept of flowing, unstoppable energy. Both are active symbols today.

Nobel laureate, chemist Friedrich August Kekule, dreamt of the uroboros one night in the late 1890s and, on waking, conceived a new molecular structure. He described the experience vividly:

> [I saw] long rows . . . all twisting and turning in snake-like motion . . . One of the snakes had seized hold of its own tail, and the form whirled mockingly before my eyes. As if by a flash of lightning I woke. I spent the rest of the night working out the consequences of the hypothesis.

He felt that his connection to the symbol opened the doors of perception and would bring him vision and wisdom because he added: 'Let us learn to dream, gentlemen, and then perhaps we shall learn the truth.'

Even in the nineteenth-century consciousness of a European scientist, the snake acted as it had for thousands of years. Kekule's imagery of twisting serpentine shapes, of uroboric eternity, of lightening flashes, of truth to come, and of a sudden inspiration that bursts ordinary boundaries are among the most common qualities of the symbolic snake, be it Amerindian, Hindu, Christian, Aborigine or alchemist. What this book attempts to show is that, despite its polyvalence, the serpent symbol is somehow so important to the human mind that its original universal power is still at large in all our renderings. The *S*-line, and its winding control that mirrors the experience of time, fascinates yet calms the imagination and can be found within virtually every snake icon from the earliest to the latest.

Dark snake colourings. A Javan wart snake, from an 1860s Austrian illustrated atlas of amphibians.

1 Living Snake

A primordial species, millions of years in existence, the snake has an almost surreal adaptability to conditions, temperatures and terrains because its compact system adjusts well, making it able to live virtually everywhere except in extreme cold.

The exact evolution of snakes is unclear, but fossils indicate that they evolved from the lizard that scuttled among the Jurassic dinosaurs 180 million years ago. This theory is supported by the vestigial pelvis and hind limbs still apparent in the skeletons of primitive species such as blindsnakes and boas. As it developed burrowing skills, the snake seems to have shed its cumbersome legs to make a swift, unmolested life for itself underground. A fossil found in Argentina dates a serpentine skeleton with lizard skull characteristics at approximately 100 million years, in the Mesozoic era, when snakes are known to have truly slithered into the world. This era's three periods – Triassic, Jurassic, and Cretaceous – produced a massive surge in all living forms. During the Triassic, water covered three-fourths of the earth except for Pangea, a vast island in the southern hemisphere made from a jammed conglomerate of modern Asia, Europe, Africa, Australia and the Americas. During the early Jurassic, Pangea divided into the northern Laurasia and the southern Gondwanaland; the latter is from where snakes are thought to have first radiated. It was still a reptilian world though a few mammals, such as rodents, existed.

The snake, with an elongated body, intense sensory organs, extremely truncated limbs and tiny eyes, commenced true life in the revolutionary Cretaceous. This period, which began 130 million years ago, encompassed enormous global change. The climate cooled. The ichthyosaur, Tyrannosaurus Rex and other dinosaurs disappeared, leaving behind newer reptiles like turtles and snakes to join the surviving crocodiles and lizards. The basis of modern animal life began. Mammal and sea life became complex. The two continents broke into many pieces. Swamps lined their shores. Flowering trees, such as the magnolia and dogwood, blossomed, and beech, fig, elm, willow and oak thrived in what would become the Americas. Grasses spread around the world. Two still living serpent species – the pipesnake and the boa – emerged.

The snake's evolution is odd – the lizard became a burrowing lizard, which became a burrowing snake, which became an above-ground snake – but it was in the 'Age of Snakes', 23 million years ago, that the snake rapidly diversified. By the Pliocene epoch, the contemporary ophidian family tree had thoroughly branched out, a completion that occurred almost 2 million years before the first recognizable modern human. This hominoid, known by her skeleton and named 'Lucy', a one-metre (three-foot) high, upright pre-Australopithecus, whose remains were found in Ethiopia, lived about 3.5 million years ago. Her species were similar to but not part of *Homo sapiens*. When Lucy was alive, barely more than half the size of a contemporary person, still covered with body hair and using only sticks and flints as tools, the snake had already become the animal it is today, its major features so perfected that only a few modifications were still to come.

There are three basic snake classifications: Cholophidia, Scolecophidia and two kinds of Alethinophidia. A second identifying category is made through the teeth – the most primitive snakes have blunt, uniform teeth and the most advanced have needle-thin, venomous fangs. Cholophidia includes all extinct fossil snakes. Scolecophidia could be said to be the living extension of that extinct group as its snakes are profoundly primitive. It represents only 300 types, known as blindsnakes, shiny burrowers shaped like worms, without a clearly delineated head and virtually sightless eyes sunk into a heavy skull that carries very few teeth. (A strange detail about this insect eater is its relationship to the screech owl. The owl will take a blindsnake to the nest to delouse it and leave the serpent there unharmed until the fledglings have grown.) All other snakes belong to the aboveground Alethinophidia. The most rudimentary class is the sunbeam snake, a true go-between between the first genus and the second. Its head is vaguely delineated and it burrows like the blindsnake but constricts like its family member, the boa, a slightly more sophisticated animal. The well-known boa, anaconda and python are large primordial snakes with delineated head shapes and unvarying teeth. They squeeze their prey to death and, like all snakes, swallow it whole, but this process is a great liability. The fight can leave them badly damaged and their digestion is slow, making them sluggish and vulnerable. Thus they eat only two to four times a year. Venomous snakes, able to strike, withdraw and digest food quickly, are free of these difficulties. The next major Alethinophidia category incorporates them and other improved snakes: the Viperidae, containing pitless vipers, such as puff adders, and pit vipers, such as rattlesnakes, bushmasters and habus; the Elapidae, which cover the cobras, mambas, and coral snakes as well as aquatic snakes such as kraits and taipans; and the Colubridae, the most typical snake, with many harmless species such as the garter, king and grass snake but also the deadly boomslang.

Snakes native to central Europe, in a 19th-century German print.

There is a balance of extinction and the unknown on either side of these categories. Almost two hundred species are currently endangered due to persecution, pollution and destruction of their terrains. But many species probably also remain undiscovered.

As an archaic animal, the snake's biological system might be expected to be simple but in fact it is complex, with a number of special oddities, some of which science has yet to fathom. Snakes have basic features such as one lung, an acute sense of smell, ectothermic energy, replaceable skins and vibrational hearing, but some details are even more intriguing, such as irregular blood pressures within the same circulation. Their bodies vary wildly – anacondas can weigh 250 kg (550 lb) and threadsnakes 3 gm (0.1 oz) – as do their singular talents such as spontaneous bleeding, cloning, under-sand breathing, and the production of complicated venoms. Even freakish, two-headed snakes are not that unusual; many zoos have them. One head controls and the other requires no care.

A snake's life span is from 10 to 50 years but is impossible to truly ascertain. Like other primordial animals, such as sharks and turtles, there is no way to detect their age. They don't grow grey, slow down or become obviously infirm. But, in a sense, snakes experience time in strange extremes. Just as the cosmic snake is about time, the natural snake is also a peculiarly temporal being. Compared to other animals, snakes are both unusually quick and unusually slow. Some snakes can strike faster than the eye can see, at 35 km an hour (22 mph), injecting a venom that shatters the nervous or circulatory system in minutes. They move on their bellies deftly and can reach speeds of up to 14 km an hour (9 mph). Conversely, a snake's digestion can be so laboured, some will eat only once a year (a record in captivity is three years without food!) and some snakes impregnate

A two-headed snake found by a Spanish farmer in 2002.

Some Australian *Colubridae* snake-head types.

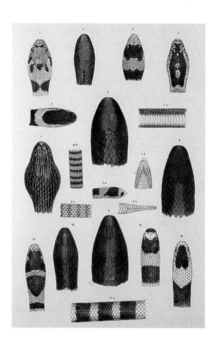

as late as two years after sex. Group sex among snakes can last for weeks. In hibernation, often two thirds of a year, the snake is moribund.

Their senses have adapted in interesting ways. Their ability to smell is acutely sensitive but is not via the nose. Rather it is located in their Jacob's organ, a tiny fluid-filled chamber, which sits in the roof of mouth near the nostrils. The organ detects odours, in concordance with the tongue, which continually darts in and out of a small permanently open area at the tip of its snout. The tongue, split at its end into a fork, picks up scent particles from the air. How the data is transferred is still not clearly understood, but the system is highly effective. A snake can catch an ant's odour even a week after it has departed. The snake is virtually deaf, but hears, with great feeling, through its jaw muscles, which pick up vibrations from the ground. These waves are conducted to the inner ear via the stapes, a delicate transmitter loosely attached below the cranium. New research suggests an even stranger conduit, in that the lung seems to play a part in how noise is filtered.

Snakes' eyes, permanently open, are covered by a transparent scale or 'spectacle'. Their sight is good and their retina operates as a zoom lens to move in and out (other kinds of eyes, humans' included, inwardly adjust the retina's shape). Some have modern technology at their scale tips such as an infrared heat sensor. This unique feature is the pit organ, lying between the nostril and the eye, and is found in pit vipers, such as rattlesnakes and habus. This organ senses warmth and finds prey in inky darkness with pinpoint accuracy. Many pythons and some boas have this feature, appearing as labial pits, vertical openings above the upper lip. The single serpent lung has a wondrous versatility, especially in water or sand snakes. All snakes can swim, and oceans, rivers and swamps harbour many species, both deadly and benign. Lithe sea snakes, such as kraits, are able to submerge for 30 minutes without breathing by sealing

An anonymous 16th-century gouache sketch of a sea-snake, with other marine animals.

A fanciful snake and alligator battle, from Maria Sibylla Merian's celebrated study of the wildlife of Surinam in the 1690s.

their nostrils with flaps. Their one lung is two-chambered, both parts hollow to store oxygen. They have conquered the corrosive effects of salt water through a gland under the tongue that expels brine and so keeps their bodies' salt concentration below that of the sea. Some desert snakes can breath under sand.

All snakes are carnivorous and must catch their food. To survive physically or psychologically (as in captivity), a snake will shrink its stomach and dull its appetite, going without for months, sometimes years. When it does eat, the snake consumes unlikely volumes by unhinging its jaw at the sides and at the front. Its jawbones, in four pieces, free float within a skull that loosely surrounds a contained brain case. This construction enables it to swallow animals whole as the bones, held together by ligaments, will separate and the mouth expand. Snakes breathe while swallowing, which can take up to six hours, through a special pipe that extends far into the front of mouth. Hard material, from eggshells to hooves, is expelled. Folktales about the meals of giant snakes are plentiful. Latin America is full of stories of horses and cows eaten by mammoth anacondas, as is Africa regarding gluttonous pythons. Out of 2,700 types of snake, the longest has been known to stretch to 9 metres (30 ft), but supersnakes are always sighted. In the early 1900s, British explorer Percy Fawcett insisted that he'd killed an 18-metre (60-ft) anaconda. Brazilian natives have described 24-metre (80-ft) ones, even testifying to trails some 2 m (6 ft) wide. In 2004, an Indonesian zoo's boast of a 15-metre (50-ft) python caused a front-page uproar. But it was a hoax. The snake was only 6.5 m (21 ft). Nevertheless, there are remarkable cases on record, such as that of an adult leopard found in the stomach of a 5.5-metre (18-ft) long rock python.

A snake's genitals are hidden in the body and activate when it smells out a mate. When looking for sex, their special vomeronasal organs detect pheromones emitted from tiny glands in the snake's back. A male and female copulate after curling around each other and tapping heads and when their tails twist together, the male's hemipenes, a forked penis, which is inside out, unfolds and enters the female's cloaca where her hemiclitoris or forked clitoris lies. Snakes can mate in groups of up to fifty, an act called 'balling,' and stay in this lump for as long as four weeks. But, even in snakes that hibernate in groups, singular sex is common. Individual snakes connect immediately before or immediately after hibernation when males battle for females by coiling round each other like braided rope and pushing to knock the other off balance, a combat dance seen in many species. They rarely bite and Mexican folklore makes copulation after the fight into a courtship by holding that rattlesnakes politely remove their fangs before sex so no harm will come to each other.

All of these qualities are surprising but the effect of heat on snakes is perhaps the most strange. It is the great determinate in their lives. It rules their bodies, their skills and their genders.

Jacopo Ligozzi,
Horned vipers and
an Avicennes
viper, chalk and
gouache on
paper.

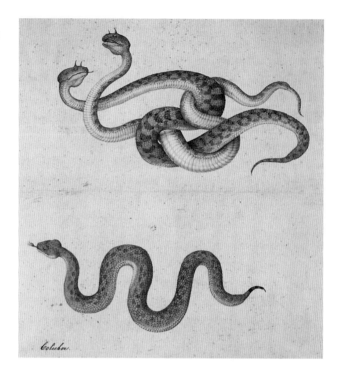

Though highly adaptable, snakes are fragile and conform to very set patterns in their unusual systems. They must stay with a temperature range of 4–38°C (39–100°F); a variation of a few degrees can kill the snake or its young. Supple and tepid to the touch, snakes are not cold blooded as is commonly assumed but ectothermic, deriving heat from outside sources, a very economical, energy-efficient means, something akin to solar panels. They warm themselves in the sun and cool themselves in shade or water to ensure the regularity of their bodies. Because of this, their blood pressure differs within areas of circulation, unique processes that are another ophidian mystery. When temperatures are low, snakes hibernate for up to eight months a year, alone or sharing a den, which may or may not mix species. Snakes have another kind of heat susceptibility: it fixes their gender. The sex of the foetus is determined by temperature: high heat creates males and moderate heat females.

Snakes are born live, hatched or cloned. At least two species of blindsnake are parthenogenetic, that is they reproduce without intercourse; all are female and the young are spontaneously produced within their bodies. Some snakes are viviparous and give birth to live young, but most, about three-fourths, are oviparous, or egg laying. This is because pregnancy makes the mother vulnerable (snakes rarely feed while pregnant) and egg laying is safer. But this varies even within a given species. For example, in the same family, Boidae, boas give birth but pythons lay eggs. But it could be said that all snakes lay eggs because the viviparous, who typically live in cooler climates and find warm nesting difficult, simply retain the eggs in the body to regulate heat. The young 'hatch' internally to emerge as live beings. Eggs develop within weeks or months then are laid in shallows or underground and covered with leaves or the like to hide and warm them. The white, oblong egg is leathery and a disposable tooth on the snout of a newborn has to cut through the tough shell. As a snake is by and large a solitary animal, and virtually fends for itself from birth, including an ability to bite venomously, most mothers leave the eggs once they emerge, even if the incubation is long. A boomslang egg, which takes six months to hatch, is immediately deserted. Conversely, the python remains with her eggs (sometimes up to a hundred), coiling around them in a heap with her head lying on top. Even though nesting can take three months, she stays like this throughout, with rare forays to drink. To fix the temperature, she twitches to generate heat or loosens her hold to circulate

A 19th-century diagram showing viviparous snake's birth: first eggs lie in the womb, then the young are born live.

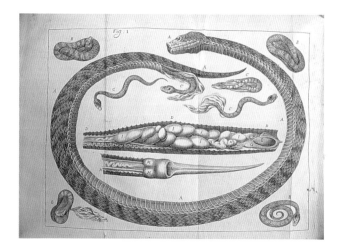

Albino Burmese python eggs hatching.

Watery boa markings.

cool air. But not all incubations take months. Other species, such as the smooth green snake, hatch their young in a few days.

A snake sheds its skin within ten days of birth. Subsequently, the skin will slough, through ecdysis, every two or three months as the body outgrows it and the skin becomes too tight. The snake hides during this difficult time, while the clear scale that covers its eye becomes milky, signifying the skin is ready for removal. As the eye clears, the skin loosens and the snake rubs it until it peels like a stocking down a leg, revealing a lustrous new layer. Even deep ocean snakes shed by rolling on top of the water.

Though often gorgeous, colouring is simply the snake's primary protection, allowing it to blend into vibrant green leaves, sunlit waves or speckled rocks with astonishing invisibility. Albinos, though not that rare, often die without this protection. Some snakes hitchhike on the camouflage of others; venomous snakes' warning colours, such as the bright red, yellow and black-banded coral snake, have allowed a number of non-lethal

A coiled boa constrictor, from an 1860s illustrated atlas of amphibians.

top right The bright markings of the coachwhip snake.

The lethal coral snake's distinctive warning colours.

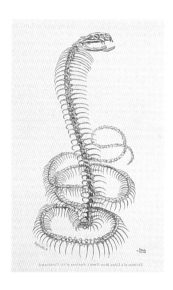

copycat snakes to live undisturbed. But snakes have desperate defences, which they use as a last resort. Some species will break their tails off between vertebrae despite the fact that, unlike the lizard tail, it cannot regenerate. Some snakes, even cobras, feign death by flopping onto their backs and letting their mouths hang open. Others roll into a very tight ball, coiled around the head as much as possible. Others exude a sticky stink, smear themselves with their faeces or emit a foul musk from a gland in their tails. Still others effect a sudden bleeding throughout their body as a means to frighten a predator. Others, like the rattlesnake, warn with a sound.

Speed is another of the snake's odd conquests. Despite having as many as 400 vertebrae, snakes move rapidly. They roll their bodies in a vertically propelled S-formation so that it undulates forward by a reticulation of muscles, similar to an accordion's movement, but one that only periodically touches

An anaconda in the process of swallowing a small deer.

the ground. Others side-wind, lilting across unusually hot surfaces like desert sand, by a series of waves that place the weight on different parts of the body and propel it horizontally. Even the sluggish can move abruptly. The Latin American anaconda, the world's largest snake, though very heavy, is known for its lightning-fast ambush.

What a creation! This seemingly simple, limbless, soft-bodied creature has somehow built itself a life of mystery and versatility. As if all these biological realties didn't astonish enough, the snake carries the most elaborate symbolism of any animal, and the mythic serpent outdoes the living snake with its vast range of talents and its extremes.

2 Mythic Snake

The universe's most powerful force in myths of Europe, Africa, the Americas, Australia and Asia, the snake has been revered as the world's creator and condemned as its destroyer. It has symbolized female and male, solar and lunar, good luck and bad luck, redeemer and devil, chaos and order, death and life, well-being and corruption. Typically the snake is themed around time, water, female divinity, resurrection, sexual vitality, trees, health, gold, evil, communication and primordial force. In ancient and prehistoric times, the serpent was creation itself. It was the dynamic of the universe, avatar of all-pervading energy, an incarnation and a conductor. To the ancient Greeks, it was a chthonic icon. To the Central American Maya, it was a Vision Serpent. To the South African Bantu it is the *chikonembo,* a forbearer reborn, and to the Swazi it is the *emadloti,* envoy between dead and living. The American Hopi and Pentecostal Christians still contact the divine through snakes. Nigerians still elicit help from snake-ancestors. Occultists still call the psychic world the 'astral snake'.

The snake may well be the first symbol. Zigzag lines, apparent in Neanderthal settlements, probably signify water but, since this image later becomes a stock serpent sign, it is possible to interpret them as snakes. From its earliest myth, the serpent, almost without exception across the world, represented time as the *essence of life* itself: as Primal Water and its tangent, the Elixir of Immortality; as a world creator and its motive of birth; or as the ascension of resurrection. Always omnipotent, the cosmic snake had two functions: to channel or to block. The channelling snake bridged worlds: potential to manifest, mundane to divine, living to dead, lower to higher. The blocking snake revelled in obstructing these processes. The serpent caused or prevented but always played the pivotal growth role.

The polyvalence of snake symbolism, though unusually contradictory, is replete with fusions. In antiquity opposites were unified in ways unimaginable today. Prehistoric observations of counter-couplings, such as death–life or water–fire, initiated dialectical cosmogonies where opposites were not polarities but working frictions that galvanized the universe. Without their grist all was static. In many religions, the snake personified this cosmic synergy. Heracleitus, in the sixth century BC, summed up the universal flux as a serpent where opposites conjoin. This philosophy of inter-relation may be the base for the snake's other great purpose: resurrection. Resurrection, the transfiguration of the dead into the living, could be said to express the moment in the synchronization of opposites where each dies (in conflict with its antithesis) and life itself is generated. The snake appears as a resurrection symbol throughout history because its presence, while *being* time, also usurped time's linearity and became a dimension in which ineffable mutation took place. As both primitive creationism *and* its theoretical progression into spiritual rebirth, the serpent bridges the two, perhaps allowing the latter to emerge as an idea.

But as societies changed, as governing powers shifted, as myths were embellished, forgotten, retold, translated and imported, the symbolism of the serpent became increasingly complex and its contradictions black and white, no longer simply ambiguous. What is fascinating about serpent mythology is that so little from its mixed bag has been completely obliterated and concepts from one culture can appear in a diluted but telling form in another, at times hundreds of years apart. These ideas have drifted, over centuries, with migrations and been reinterpreted by opportunists or overcome by the self-righteous, yet many echoes of the snake's supernal reign in antiquity remain even today. The snake is still venerated. The snake is still sexual. The snake is still the devil. The snake is still time. The snake is still water. The snake is still a conduit. Long after its sovereignty as the cosmic flux in archaic times, the serpent can be glimpsed, internationally, for centuries, tacitly underpinning innumerable attempts to grasp the metaphysical. Process, transmutation and the melding of disparate realities remain the legacy of the symbolic snake even today, a phenomenon that Kekule's unconscious tapped only a hundred years ago.

There is logic to these seemingly bizarre meanings. The snake's discarded skin signified immortal life; its access to, and return from, the underground suggested mobility between upper and lower realms and thus a secret knowledge of the dead; its fatal venom mimicked supernatural power and became a force of evil; its venom's use as an antidote to venom made the snake, killing and curing at once, a perfect blend of oppositions; its limbless versatility gave it a spirit quality; its graceful beauty was beguiling; its gigantic mouth that swallowed creatures whole mirrored a maw of damnation or resurrection; its swift motion, coiling strength and lightning strikes signalled astounding life energy; its dexterity in all elements showed universal control; its curled shape matched the spiral, emblem of the swirling cosmos and of endless eternity; its body movement and its body were one machine, making it a signature of action itself; its primordial, enduring biology, combined with all the above, made it the obvious choice to incarnate the cosmos.

This incarnation has two stages of mythology: first, the prehistoric and archaic serpent, perceived as a whole being profuse with protean talents, and second, the ancient and latter day serpent, whose grandeur is piecemeal and hidden, broken up into specific qualities. But it is clear that the vast ontology of the original serpent still infuses the modern.

COSMIC SNAKE

The cosmic snake is about time. It begins in the Palaeolithic as a seasonal image, enters pre-recorded history as a creator animal and evolves into philosophies of creation as an ongoing process. In the earliest stories, the snake represents undifferentiated duration manifested as water, where life began and through which life continues. The uroboros, probably the most recognized serpent symbol today, is one of the first to concretize this meaning. Just as time swallows the past, the uroboros eats its own tail in unending consumption. Found in African spiritualism, European alchemy, Buddhism, Hinduism and ancient Greek and Egyptian faiths, and always associated with eternity, the image could go back to the Palaeolithic when time was first conceived in cosmological terms. A matriarchal culture and a matristic religion, with an Earth Mother deity now referenced as the Great Goddess, is likely to have begun in this era as its presence proliferates in the Neolithic and the first sacred art forms, from over 25,000 years ago, depict a goddess character. The sinuous snake, living in consecrated water, caves, trees, mountains and the subterranean, was the Goddess's elemental proxy. This faith lasted, unrivalled, until the fourth millennium BC.

Erich Neuman, in *The Great Mother*, argues that as a uroboric sign, the snake encapsulates the 'Great Round' of the Great Goddess. Her pregnant belly or the fully contained, ever conceiving, cosmic and physical world, is the meld of destruction and creation which manifests transformation. This conceptual uroboros *is* multi-dimensional time, mixing inner, outer, lower, upper and process within process, creating the most symbiotic of all concepts, that of a 'participation mystique' in a communally generative universe.[1] Alexander Marshack, in *The Roots of Civilization*, a ground-breaking investigation of prehistoric culture, argued that the advanced science, art, law and religion visible in societies by the fourth millennium, originated with Upper Paleolithic tribes whose grasp of time is evident in their counting systems and toolmaking and whose art shows a genius for the ideal. Out of this broad consciousness the cosmic snake was born, riding the nascent creation myths.

Snakes rarely appear in cave murals but are found on artefacts unearthed in Europe. Some of these are long, moulded, snake-like bones, cut with figures or marks, and occasionally a hole in one end, and show the wear of much handling, as if passed down through generations, yet they are not tools. Marshack argues that these bones are calendars with line and dot decorations that track six or more months of moon phases. Some, impressed with red ochre typical of ritual use, were probably ceremonial objects kept by shamans. Others depict mythic scenes. One such, 15,000 years old, shows a straight, plump snake, with geometric skin and a vivid forked tongue, sliding between plants and wide-eyed bird heads. Marshack suggests that bird and snake conjoin sky and earth and that spring fertility is evoked if the birds are chicks and the snake pregnant. Another etched bone, marked with horizontal lines, portrays a giant snake floating behind a sketchy male figure who carries a

branch on his shoulder. These recurrent branch/plant motifs, Marshack points out, were often linked to the 'ritualized or symbolized' snake and 'played a part in a range of ceremonies or myths'.[2] This combination of snake/branch/plant continues well into antiquity. One of the most prominent is the Biblical snake and the Tree of the Knowledge of Good and Evil.

Though snakes are not painted in caves, wavy, zigzag or serpentine lines are common and the serpentine line, as an abstraction, could be said to have first appeared here in a universal context. A twelfth-millennium artefact known as the Taï plaque, a tiny reindeer bone found in Europe, has a set of symbolic marks which may be designed around an internal serpent theme. The lines seem to be a boustrophedon, that is, meant to be read in one continuous seam. The marks seem to begin at the left and, at the next line, be patterned to be read from right to left. The next line reverts to left-right and so on. This creates a serpentine linearity and thus continuity for the reading eye. These markings may record lunar phases. However, breaks inset within them suggest solar equinoxes and solstices and Marshack concludes that this object was both a lunar and solar calendar.[3]

The use of a boustrophedon line is speculative but raises a provocative idea. A serpent-like image made during a period when the snake was an important symbol must be consequential. It could be said that this iconography is designed to resemble a theoretical cosmic serpent. Almost every later cosmology takes a snake to represent the universe and this subtle image may be one of its first manifestations. In the Taï plaque, the serpentine line, waving through the marks that note the passing of a solar and lunar world, beautifully expresses the concept of 'continuing'. Its S-shape, which encompasses time as a seasonal structure, offers time also as an idea. As such it adheres time, cosmology, science, art and the snake in ways that anticipate and even surpass the narrativized creation serpent to come.

PRIMAL CHAOS

This imaginative history precedes the written epic myths of the Primal Chaos Snake, which appeared throughout the world around five thousand years ago. A snake's natural features, inviting metaphors of agelessness, quickness and transformation, made it a clear choice for its two archaic roles. One was as the Primal Water or Chaos, typically rendered as a gigantic snake wherein all undivided substance sloshed. Death and birth blurred. All was potential. The other role was the universal energizer, which awakened possibility into being. In some cases, these concepts develop in sophistication over thousands of years (as through the practice of kundalini, a yogic art), in others they devolve through politics (as in the combat myth), as discussed below, but they provide for all serpent symbolism to come.

Directly or through implication, this snake was female or male, a blend of both or a superimposition of two deities, one historically older than the other. Often a male had a female precursor; sometimes maleness was allotted to a female serpent to make it a worthier foe of a male hero. This layering is core to early philosophy. Anthropologist Marija Gimbutus, a pioneer in Neolithic studies, stresses that in the Neolithic, 'female and male sexes were not dichotomized . . . on the contrary, it was believed that fusing their created potency was necessary to charge nature with its life powers'.[4] Some speculate that this fusion was divided, making the male creation snake a phallic tool for the uterine female creatrix. Though Neuman sees the uroboros, personifying time as conception, as the emblem par excellence of the female cosmic agency, he and others such as mythologist Joseph Campbell also identify the snake as a consort. Neuman suggests that 'as the underground water [the snake] fecundates her womb; or else it may represent the upper and celestial water, the *nous*-spirit serpent that enters into the feminine soul and guides it'.[5] Others, such as mythologists Barbara Walker, Barbara Mor and Monica Sjöö, as well as Gimbutus, argue that the Goddess holds the inferred phallus within her. The oldest creation myths uphold the latter as in them the ophidian female jumpstarts an impassive male quintessence, an energy sublimely portrayed in the Hindu concept of Sakti, discussed below. True gender separation appeared in the ordination of kingship, commencing social hierarchy, where the royal man 'married' the Goddess, often a bloody relationship. In Greece, these consort-kings, as incarnations of the daimonic (always female) urge were viewed *as* snakes (the time animal) and killed or usurped after a nine year cycle.[6] Similar sacrifices occurred in Asia. Some consorts, in Central America and the Middle East, lived but participated in self-mutilation.

Creation usually begins in a watery cosmos almost invariably animalized as a snake. The earliest stories have no progenitor spirit, only the mingling of opposites through their sameness. The Sumerian *Enuma elish*, the world's oldest extant text, written about 3100 BC, describes pre-creation as a two-fold liquid domain. The male Apsu was sweet (fresh) water and Tiamat, the Great Mother Serpent of Heaven, was bitter (salt) water. Tiamat, as the epic's opening cited her ('She who gave birth to them all'), brought Apsu into being. They bore Mummu (the waves or Confusion) and two serpent monsters, which bore the sky and earth that bore the gods. The earliest Egyptian creation texts recount a like tale of a dark, fluid primal sky mixture of the (typically) snake-headed male, Nu, and snake-headed female, Nut. The universe, sun god and divine pantheon were born from their coupling. As a primeval mother deity, Nut was always crowned with a disc and her importance was underscored by her survival as the sky divinity in classical Egyptian mythology (though Nu disappeared). A few thousand years later, the Judaeo-Christian book of Genesis cited a similar creation between Tehom, the 'face of the deep' (a version of Tiamat), and the moving 'spirit'.

By the time of the Hindu *Vedas*, the third millennium scripture of the Indus Valley Dravidians and their Aryan colonizers, the cosmos, though built along the old origin myth principles, sustained a more defined male. Creation was ongoing, taking place over billions of cycles, and the time snake combined the masculine Aryan and the feminine Dravidian. The Supreme Absolute was Vishnu, the god who sleeps the sleep of potential, from aeon to aeon, while lying 'in the lap of the serpent',[7] which was both the snake Sesa (meaning 'Remainder') and the thousand-headed snake Ananta (meaning 'Endless'). Like Apsu and Nu, Vishnu was inert until charged with life. Ananta was both cosmic water and Vishnu's avatar and, though at times male, was primarily a serpent-mother who cradled him and the other gods during their potent, death-like phases. S/he is eternity, holding growth and potential in one unending span. At the close of each cycle, s/he apocalyptically burns the universe. Remainder, on the other hand, is temporality, the sway of death and life, and he presides over both the Underworld and the Nagas, snakes representing time's cycles. Hindu scholar Jean Danielou reveals that, by 2000 BC, the cosmic time serpent had evolved from a creation animal to a phenomenological body *of* the resurrection process itself:

> [T]he serpent represents the non-evolved form of Nature, the totality of the causal stage of consciousness, the eternity of time's endless revolutions. . . . When creation is withdrawn it cannot entirely cease to be; there must remain in a subtle form the germ of all that has been and will be so that the world may rise again.[8]

Here, the serpent body holds (and thus *is*) continuity, a temporal reality, which is translated as sacred rejuvenation. The snake expresses the principle of reviviscence, present everywhere and in everything. It is the ineluctable symbiosis between seed to flower, unconscious to idea, and past to future; it is the fact that the old is always the substratum of the new.

Pre-Hellenic Greece contrived a more theatrical creation myth, far cruder than the older *Vedas*, but Gimbutus and historian Robert Graves argue that this is because it is actually a Neolithic story. In it, the Universal One, Eurynome, rose from Primordial Water, separated sea and sky, and created and copulated with the wind serpent, Ophion. Out of the egg of their union gushed forth sun, moon, planets and living earth. When the serpent claimed credit, Eurynome kicked out his teeth and banished him to the underworld. Here the male snake, clearly a consort, is explicitly a phallic emanation of the creatrix womb. The Christian Gnostics believed similarly that their Mother of Creation, Sophia, 'infused' Jehovah with energy. When he appropriated the change as his own she also punished him. This adds a serpent's ghost to representations of Jehovah.

Many later myths around the world reverberate with these time fundamentals of water, regeneration, activation and

destruction. The Guinean Baga's creation serpent also excited Primal Water and slashed across the earth to disperse it. The Algonquian's creator is Manitou, the lightning flashing serpent. The Venezuelan Yaruros' creator is Puana, a snake. Una, the All-Mother of the Aboriginal Australians, whose cosmology is based on the Rainbow Snake, made heaven and earth and always holds the cosmic snake in her arms. The Chinese dragon guardian of pools and ocean extends from the cosmic snake that brings vivifying rain, good fortune and holy sanction. The Dahomey world serpent, Dan Ayido Hwedo, another Rainbow Snake, carried the Creator in its mouth while the world was formed, making mountains of excrement so heavy (though filled with gold) that the Creator asked it to become a uroboros and hold up the world from under the ocean. If it is not continuously fed, it will eat its tail causing, like the Hindu Ananta, the world to misalign and disintegrate. Another spin on creation may lie with the astronomically aligned Amerindian Serpent

Mound, in Ohio, made during the eleventh century, which is moulded out of earth, for a quarter mile, into the winding curls of a long snake (whose mouth is on an egg) such that the shape 'couples' with the terrain.

The snake's body as a place of transformation from disorder to order (or order to disorder) could be said to be the dominant theme of ophidian symbolism. Just as Ananta holds both potential and manifestation, the serpent is internationally fabled as a being out of which social precepts grow. The Malian Dogon creation myth ingeniously portrays this concept of a cosmological base that manifests a cultural system. For the Dogon, the snake's living matter was a shamanistic conductor through which societal structure was introduced (a theme echoed in Mayan beliefs, as discussed below). After the eight original families had been made, the oldest man, who represented the Word, needed to enact a ritual death. The seventh ancestor became a snake, swallowed him, and vomited out stones into a human outline. These stones, passed down through generations, became the linchpins of cultural institutions, symbolizing the cinching of opposites (especially marriage). The snake's swallowing changed non-order into order, showing that in the body (the serpent as the swallowed man), the one transformed into the other. The two stages were always unified in a single substance, a single whole.

SNAKE GODDESS

With the development of cities, the generic Great Goddess was delineated into, among others, the Snake Goddess of the Neolithic era (c. 9000–6000 BC). Her immediate ancestor was the Snake and Bird Goddess, inheritor of the Palaeolithic bird-serpent. The frequent egg-shapes of that period evolved into stylized snake and egg patterns in the Neolithic and, in iconography across Europe, the Snake and Bird Goddess appeared as a world egg or two eggs, usually wound by snakes, a motif much passed on (as evidenced in the Eurynome tale). These very images return centuries later in the icons of the Orphic Mysteries and the Gnostic world egg.

The Snake and Bird Goddess ruled as late as pre-dynastic (sixth to fourth millennium BC) Egypt (where snake religion had long been established) as the twin Uatcheti sisters. Though few details of their worship remain, they were clearly creation deities, originating law, healing and agriculture, whose authority was signified by a long papyrus sceptre entwined with a hood-extended cobra. Lower Egypt (Northern) revered Uatchet (or Wadjyt), the Cobra Goddess, called 'lady of heaven, mistress of all the gods'. Upper Egypt (Southern) revered Nekhebt, the Vulture Goddess, the 'form of the primeval abyss which brought forth light', the 'creatrix of the world', known as 'father of fathers, mother of mothers, who have existed from the beginning'.[9] The Cobra Goddess dominated and, long before the Pyramid Texts were written (mid-third millennium BC), morphed into the next 'mistress of all the gods', Isis. She was also identified with Thoth (god of writing, magic and healing, later appropriated by medieval alchemy), with Hathor (archaic precursor to Isis and vengeful eye of Ra) and even Horus (the sun god). Though absorbed into later pantheons, the Uatcheti were irreplaceable in Egyptian consciousness and became Ra's supernal eyes during his underworld journey. They protected his disc, which, like the world egg, was circled by a serpent, and their emblematic cobra head or uraeus, sign of sacred authority, crested the crown for three thousand years. Thus, as a uraeus, the Uatcheti remained on Ra's forehead, their rightful place. A late Snake and Bird Goddess appeared as the Sumerian

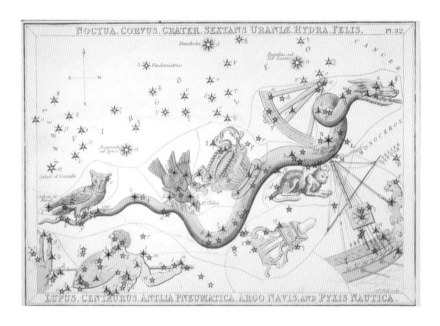

A hand-coloured etching of the constellation of Hydra, from an 1825 *Familiar Treatise on Astronomy*.

Lilith who possessively squatted between the Zu-bird (in branches) and the snake (in roots) of a divine tree until chased away. She transmogrified, centuries later, into the Talmudic Lilith who preceded Eve as Adam's mate and whose woman's body had taloned feet, whose hands often held snakes and who was considered a child eater and succubus.

Though the prehistoric Snake and Bird Goddess merged into the Neolithic Snake Goddess, bird and snake symbolism has not died out. Imagery of bird versus snake prevailed in Babylonian and Polynesian mythology. The Mayan cosmic Tree held a celestial bird and had serpent limbs. The Nordic Tree, Yggdrasil, was tormented by a fight between an eagle in its branches and a serpent, Nidhogg, gnawing at its roots, as was Southern Borneo's Tree, with its female serpent below warring

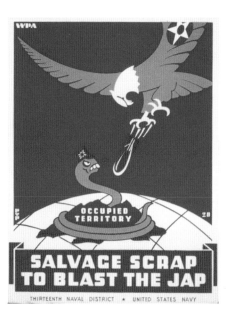

A Second World War poster with the USA as an eagle attacking Japan as a snake.

with the male eagle above. In India, Garudas, or bird deities, fight the Nagas, serpent deities. In Mexico, the national flag bears an eagle struggling with a snake. In nineteenth-century Europe, Friedrich Nietzsche, in *Thus Spake Zarathustra*, harnessed this ancient, co-ordinate enmity by taking the bird and snake as symbols of strength and opposition for his Superman's attributes. They are still used as combative equals in a variety of contexts.

The Neolithic Snake Goddess reigned in an era when society, from the tenth millennium to the seventh, radicalized the world. A tremendous creativity emerged as the first cities were built, first crops propagated, first animals tamed and a new industrial revolution, with inventions such as the loom, initiated. The labyrinth, mound and cone, some of the earliest sacred structures,

Centuries after its first Neolithic sexual imagery, the snake, as life energy, still infuses the genitals in this *c.* 10th-century sculpture from Mexico.

all associated with the serpent, developed as architecture. Under this drive toward the concrete lay the marvellous Neolithic affinity for the abstract, able to comfortably render philosophical ideas as graphic images. They were especially deft at figurations of time, be it duration ('becoming') or quantum ('universal dynamism'). Again, snakes or eggs were the means of expression. Becoming was an egg within a human buttock, conjuring gestation but set in the imaginary (its anomalous place). The dynamic was a pair of rampant snakes whose coils made, as Gimbutus puts it, 'the world roll'.[10]

The snake and its spiral was the era's preponderant symbol, repeatedly combined with egg, disc, zigzag and dot patterns. Snakes were painted in orange, black, red and white on every

Neolithic Snake Goddess figurine with (red) Kundalini stripes, from Anatolia, c. 6,000 BC.

kind of surface, walls, furniture, dishes, hearths and altars and sculpted in almost three-dimensioned bas-relief on ritual pottery. The Goddess was now fashioned with snake arms or a snake head, carrying snakes, wrapped in snakes or with a body flourishing in snake spirals or winding stripes. Spirals replaced vulvas or adorned every female roundness – stomach, shoulder, buttock, breast, even knee – as well as phallic erections. The snake equalled all spontaneous life energy and Gimbutus argues that these frequent designs testify that the vulva, pregnant mound and engorged penis were the known source of conception. The snake and the reproductive spark were one.

During the seventh millennium BC, this concept was tailored into an ideology. Figurines, as crowned and/or snake-headed females, were shaped in the yogic lotus position with one leg laid upon the other, some painted with sinewy red lines. Though these figures are found primarily in Europe, Gimbutus speculates that the lines illustrate the life force as kundalini, a current coursing the body. Kundalini is the Hindu living energy, conceived as a serpent and rooted in sexual power, which lies at the base of the spine in the muladhara chakra. The ultimate yogic attainment, advanced exercise works the Kundalini serpent up the seven chakras to the head's crown to achieve highest consciousness.

Meaning 'the coiled', Kundalini named a pre-Vedic goddess venerated as the source of everything, the primal integration. Conceptualized as Sakti, the energy (always female) that animates the flux and causes the universe to live, she became the serpent in Kundalini yoga. Much as the all-encompassing uroboric Palaeolithic Great Goddess contained the universe, Sakti is immanence itself, the soma of Brahma-Vishnu-Siva, and is described in the *Vedas* as both 'Nature' (life) and 'the form of all that is conscious', the 'origin, the knowledge, the perception of reality, the instigator of the intellect'.[11] She provokes static potential, divine or mundane, corporeal or ethereal, thought or intuition, into manifestation. Without her suffusion, Siva has no function; just as Tiamat animated Apsu, Sakti rouses Siva by enveloping him as the vagina envelops the penis. Kundalini is still worshipped as a lingam (penis) surrounded by a yoni (vagina). Gimbutus's idea suggests a fascinating lineage and the Vedic debt to Neolithic thinking is clear: the snake-identified phallus and vulva, the feminized serpent energy that everlastingly combusts the immanent universe into being, and the seated body whose ritualized actions mimic, and bond with, the deeper world when its life force, the spine (paralysed if damaged), joins with the cosmic snake.

A Minoan snake-handling priestess, Crete, *c.* 1500 BC, faience.

The third millennium BC saw the greatest, and last, reign of the Snake Goddess, in one of the world's most brilliant cultures, the Cretan Minoan, whose serpent religion held together a matriarchal society of astounding advancement (with indoor drainage, four-storey buildings, complex grammar, tailored clothing and chess). With its destruction, the Snake Goddess as complete deity began to submerge, and by the second millennium BC, as civilization widened, she had diversified into numerous goddesses, gods, cults and ideologies where the snake was a recurrent avatar and symbol. But as these beliefs progressed, the millennia old ophidian connotations of water, wisdom, healing, fertility, the underworld, resurrection and immortality remained the norm.

The Mysteries, hugely popular religions thriving as late as the third century AD and stretching across the western and southern Mediterranean, through North Africa and the Middle East, internalized the Snake Goddess. The most influential faiths, Eleusian, Isis, Bacchic and Magna Mater, venerated the snake in various ways and were based in awakening consciousness by offering the initiand dissolution into the divine through secret initiation ceremonies often held at night in catacombs and caves.

The most famous were the oldest – the Eleusian Mysteries and the Mysteries of Isis. The first, well established by the sixth century BC, centred on Demeter, Mother Goddess, and her daughter Persephone, Underworld ruler, and, though central to Athenian life, was almost certainly a Neolithic holdover with probable links to the Minoans. Snakes, emblems of sovereignty, life and chthonic control, often accompanied the two deities. The Mysteries of Isis, begun in Egypt but widely disseminated throughout the Mediterranean, was still very strong in late antiquity and was Rome's prime Mystery religion, often banned and just as often reinstated. The Roman initiate, Apuleius, in the second century AD, wrote the only first-hand account of its secrets in *The Golden Ass*, where Isis, adorned with snakes, appears as the universal divinity. Roman amulets depicted her with a snake tail.

But snakes excelled in the Bacchic Mysteries, a 900-year-long movement devoted to the Greek god Dionysus (Bacchus). Its violent female followers, the Bacchantes, roamed the countryside, drunk on wine and mysticism, carrying snakes, biting them to pieces, or tying them around their hair and waists. In Bacchic services, the serpent was a mystic channel. In the ritual 'God through the lap', a metal snake, pulled across the initiand while she or he sat in a dim, candle lit cavern, stood in for divinity, a symbolic intercourse that was less a sexual joining than one of prosaic and heavenly union (ever the serpent's role).[12] The Orphic Mysteries, an arcane offshoot, worshipped Orpheus, who had entered Hades to retrieve, unsuccessfully, his lover poisoned by snakebite. Killed by the Bacchantes, he was a resurrection figure, probably a latter-day Dionysus or his priest, and considered a forerunner of Jesus. All Orphic rituals were constructed around a world spirit serpent.

The most vicious Mystery was the Magna Mater cult. Based in Asia Minor, it so revered the goddess Meter (or Cybele) and her annually dying consort Attis, that her priests, the frenzied Corybantes, dressed as women and castrated themselves in a desire to feign the female genital. Though not focused on serpents per se, its relation between mundane and divine and its transgender theme are repeated in later snake myths in ways worth examining. It is speculative that the androgyny of renowned Greek seer Teiresias involved him with this cult, but Hesiod's eighth-century BC account possibly relays a bastardized story of Meter's priests. Teiresias' true role is lost but the Hellenes regarded him as unparalleled. He announced Dionysus as Olympian in Euripides' fifth-century BC *The Bacchae,* revealed Oedipus' crime to him in Sophocles' *Oedipus Rex* of the same era and, though dead, advised Odysseus in Homer's ninth-century *Odyssey*. One of his stranger exploits was his transmutation into a woman after striking two copulating serpents with a stick and his return to masculinity seven years later by hitting the same couple. Though the fable seems comic, Teiresias's presence guarantees *gravitas,* suggesting that the entwined snakes, sexual union, powerful stick and woman sorcerer (Teiresias himself) are analogues for a matristic, serpentine authority.

The African Dogon connect the snake with cross-dressing in much the same way: as a demonstration of matriarchal divinity. The Dogons tell that a jackal took Mother Earth's skirt. A

A Pompeiian mural of Bacchic mysteries with a holy snake, before 79 AD.

woman stole it, wore it and became a ruler. Men seized the skirt, proclaimed themselves kings by wearing it, and banned women from this apparel. But trouble started when an old man's ignorance of this new authority caused a breach in worldly order. Consequently, when he died he became a serpent instead of a ghost and then terrorized the young skirted men. Trapped between two zones, he died again, whereupon the villagers wrapped the dead snake in the skirt and laid it in a cave. The lost man's soul entered a baby (born mottled like the snake and red like the skirt) who soon became normal. These disturbances engendered the first death rituals (to rightly settle the dead) and the first art (for correct cultural sequences).

Here again, the snake serves as resurrector and guide for the dead. The proper placement of Mother Earth's serpent, skirt and cave realigns the world. As the conduit through rebirth (as the baby) that blends dead with living and matriarchal with patriarchal, the snake composes true, revived order out of the false, usurping one. This situation, where the universal snake's body substantiates the next world, will be the basis of the combat myth, the story that heralds antiquity's most disruptive social change.

COMBAT MYTH

The combat myth follows hard on the heels of the primal myth. It re-orders the relationship between proactive serpent (female) and potential life (male) into a battle between the two, in which the roles reverse and one opponent must die. The combat myth is a genre, which like the Dogon story, recounts a change in the order of things, a handover of autocracy from matriarch to patriarch. This process began in the third and second millennia BC and the combat myth, which proliferated across the Near East, the Mediterranean and Europe, allegorized the event. Though she is concerned specifically with Greece, scholar Jane Harrison's hypothesis of how the sacred snake or Agathos Daemon, the life force, came to be murdered throws light on all combat myths. She speculates that the destructive side of the daemonic snake (as nature) and its sacrifice as the incarnated consort-king, made its death conceivable, even if never truly acceptable.[13]

Almost without exception, the combat myth features a solar hero who conquers, sometimes daily, the undivided cosmos personified as the creation snake. With his triumph, he moulds a living universe of light from the serpent's dead, dark flesh. In Egyptian, Babylonian, Greek, Persian and Hindu mythology this snake is both beneficent and maleficent: beneficent because its presence is crucial to the future; maleficent because, alive, it blocks that future's existence. The defeated snake is the old matristic culture but, as the stories reveal, its corpus, in effect its knowledge, underpins the new patristic one. Two narrative elements support this. First, the renewed world is made from the old corpse. Second, in many cases, the killing is a crime for which the hero pays an extreme, near fatal, penalty. Only penance or, as in Egypt, a synergistic daily struggle will maintain balance. Though the plot is designed as a lethal conquest, covertly the dark snake is beyond death. As the existential base of the transformed world, it is ever present and thus remains the universal process. The 'bad' snake (its old association) dies so that the 'good' snake (its powers) will rise as the new cosmos. In this sense, resurrection is truly the underlying concept. The new order is a resurrection of the old: the corpse comes alive again, under a fresh name. This theme of ophidian rejuvenation runs through history as one of the most enduring of serpentine attributes.

In the earliest mythic record, the Egyptian, the combat glories in the dialectic. Here, the serpent is not permanently defeated but is half of the ever-functioning world. The sun, Ra, warred every night with Apophis, the giant multi-coiled male serpent of the underworld. While within the female snake Mehen's protective canopy or uroboros, Ra killed Apophis daily at dawn. But the experience both exhausted and rejuvenated him. In the last black hour, his boat passed through the serpent, Ka-en-Ankh-neteru ('Life of the Gods'), and Ra emerged from its mouth, reborn, into daylight. As Egyptologist E. A. Wallis Budge describes it, Ra 'enters the snake in the form of the old Sun god, and he comes forth not only alive, but made young again'.[14]

The later combat myth eliminated this relationship and lauded a seemingly permanent victory, one ratified with the Aryan migrations. Their solar calendar overtook the old lunar one, where time was female and serpentine, and their patriarchal myths, with sky gods, thunderbolts and mountains, eclipsed the snakes, caves and water of the Goddess religion. Calling themselves 'people of the sky', they invaded India's indigenous Dravidians, an agrarian, matriarchal tribe, and excoriated them as 'people of the earth and the serpent',[15] bringing home the fatal separation between the era of the Snake Goddess and that of the Sky God. In their *Vedas*, storm god Indra slew the chaos snake, Vritra (meaning 'obstruction' or 'dark cloud'), a uroboros who imprisoned the Primal Water. In the earliest texts, Vritra assumes the female through his mother, Danu, the Dravidian Great Goddess (and snake correlative), a femininity underscored in the later *Mahabharata*, which phallicizes the lightning that devastates the snake as s/he tries to swallow Indra. Despite death, it is Vritra/Danu's blood that initiates creation. Indispensably germinal, it flows into the released Primal Waters, inseminating them until 'pregnant' with the sun. When the sun, Indra's aspect, is born, the next world appears. Though Vritra is obstructive, its blood engenders. Without it, nothing can happen. And the price of the conflict is high. In the *Puranas*, Vritra becomes a priest and Indra is forced, as punishment for the murder, to relinquish his throne. In other texts, a terrified Indra flees the killing and, nearly dead, goes to the end of the world where he endures holy expiation, after which he is saved.

A similar story crossed Northern Europe. Hurling thunderbolts, Thor, the Nordic storm god, fought the giant Midgard serpent that squeezed growth and well-being from the World Tree much as Vritra robbed the essential waters. In this eschatology, both the serpent and Thor die. The Babylonians devised a like-minded sun warrior, Marduk, to defeat the Sumerian Mother Serpent of Heaven, Tiamat. As she tried to swallow him, Marduk killed her and made earth, sea and sky from her body.

Persian Zoroastrianism's twin brothers, Ahriman, the dark Serpent, and Ahura Mazda, the light Hero, born of the androgynous Zurvann, Crone of Time, are also equals. For aeons, they equitably ruled the universe, then fought a war that Ahura Mazda only partially won. Though vanquished, Ahriman was still a requisite: his evil powered half of the universal flux. Only in the final upheaval, akin to the Christian Apocalypse, were Ahriman and the serpent Azi Dahak burned until their substance purified hell and they vanished. Their ophidian presence inaugurates and perfects the next and resurrected world.

Hellenistic snakes retained their sacred pull and stories about them, monstrous and blessed, abound, but their prominence faded with their meaning. The combat myth figures, though less strongly, probably as an allegory for earlier epistemologies or actual coups. Two dominate: Zeus versus Typhon and Apollo versus Python. The first, when sky god Zeus, escaping death, defeated the serpent Typhon, son of Gaia (Mother Earth), is thought to rework the Egyptian skirmish between resurrection god Osiris and his brother Set who, as a serpent, killed him in a bid for power. The murder, however, inaugurated Osiris as resurrection deity, reflecting, again, the necessity of the serpent, however maligned, to activate the ontological cycle of life. This same redemption from the serpent's 'evil' appeared a few centuries later in Gnostic tenets, which held that the Edenic snake's offer of knowledge matched and heralded Christ's offer of salvation. In the Greek versions, these themes were deeply buried.

The second story, in which sun god Apollo fought Python, the snake guardian (possibly a parthenogenous offspring of Hera, queen of Heaven) of the Delphic oracle, relays the Apollonian seizure of Delphi. The appropriation of this site (named for Delphyne, serpent consort of, and/or precursor to, Python) is crucial in the Hellenistic abrogation of the region's

Goddess worship. Delphi's importance must not be underestimated. The Mediterranean's most spiritual centre for centuries, its oracular women, known as Sibyl or Pythia, influenced history many times with their prophecies. The Pythia and her sacred python sat deep within the temple, at the omphalos, or 'navel of the world', where Gaia was revered as a mound or beehive. Built near a vaporous cave below Mount Parnassus, the temple was the destination of ritual steps danced in a serpentine line through a threshing floor levelled between mountain and cave, as a re-enactment of a snake birth. The Apollo-Python story is soaked in the snake's sanctification. Python's death during the Delphic coup was so heinous that Pythian funeral games were instituted there in the snake's honour. Like Indra, after the slaughter, Apollo fled his hubristic murder and performed a ritual cleansing to expiate his guilt. (In some versions, Apollo is even killed by Python and then revived.) He suffered severe penance beyond the world's limits for a set time (nine years) before being allowed to return.

In Central America, by the tenth century AD, the great Mexican Toltec deity Quetzlcoatl (Plumed Serpent), later claimed by the Aztecs, was conceived as a feathered snake and, though a non-bellicose deity, also fulfilled the combat destiny. A god version of the Snake and Bird Goddess, sun god Quetzlcoatl, reconciled earth and sky. Like the Egyptian Uatcheti, he bestowed agriculture, law, medicine, as well as learning, metallurgy, the calendar and blood sacrifice. His counterpart, Tezcatlipoca or Smoking Mirror, a trickster god of night and sorcery, incarnated resurrection and his darkness, complimenting Queztlcoatl's light, was creation's death aspect, ensuring that rebirth occurred. The twins were a working unit and they too defeated the primal female creatrix to remake the world. In the beginning all was water inhabited by Tlatecuhtli (very like

Mexican supreme Toltec and Aztec deity Queztlcoatl as a feathered serpent, c. 10th century AD.

Tiamat), a giant female (or sometimes male) cayman. Quetzlcoatl and Tezcatlipoca, (living in the sky), transformed into serpents and pulled Tlatecuhtli's body into two parts from which they made earth and heaven. But the primality of this first aqua being is preserved in the name Quetzlcoatl because 'coatl', meaning 'serpent', breaks down to 'co' (snake) and 'atl' (water), a prefix/ suffix for other divine titles.

North America's embrace of the combat myth disrupted the outcome but retained the narrative rudiments. In the beginning of time, the one-horned serpent witch Uncegila caused blindness, insanity and death by the mere sight of her. But her freezing red crystal heart was the absolute of power, rewarding its bearer with clairvoyance, perfect libidinal and hunting skill and the end of hunger. Twin brothers sought help to defeat her from 'Ugly Old Woman' in her mountain cave and she offered them advice in exchange for sex. One blind brother agreed and the woman, released from enchantment, became young and eventually disappeared. When Uncegila was killed, her blood restored the brother's sight and her heart gave the twins everything they desired. But this was so boring that they broke the heart's spell and gladly returned to their normal lives.

Even Christianity absorbed the combat myth. The Persian conquest of Babylon influenced Judaism and Ahriman is linked to Eden's serpent and to Lucifer, paving a way for the New Testament's omniscient Satan snake. In the fourth-century Nicean Creed, which established Christianity's ecumenical direction, Jesus fought the serpent (now the Devil), descended into hell (a giant mouth) for three days and was reborn, fully divine, from his experience in the underworld. There are echoes of the Apollo/Indra expiation here: defeat of a supernal snake, a set period in a severe condition (hell), and redemption as refined divinity. Jesus also fights the snake as the 'anti-Christ' of the Judaic tribe of Dan ('Dan shall be a serpent by the way, an adder in the path'). These Christian fears laced fantastic tales such as the fourteenth-century English *Lambton Worm* about Lord Lambton who, having avoided church to fish, caught a tiny 'loathsome Worm' (snake) which grew so big that it circled a hill. A 'sibyl' advised Lambton on warfare but warned of a condition: he must slaughter whoever was met after the successful fight. This was his father and Lambton's refusal to kill him initiated a curse. The story's wise woman, snake, hill and cursed killer conjure the Delphic Sibyl, her sacred mound and the Python slain by the criminalized Apollo.

In lesser versions of the genre, a hero kills the snake for its gold or secrets but the corpse still offers the murderer, as it did the god, access to a higher plane. The Greek Perseus and the Nordic Siegfried are classic examples. Perseus slew the serpent-haired demi-deity Medusa and gave the head to Athene, the goddess of

A 16th-century
Flemish oil
painting of the
Head of Medusa.

wisdom and war. That it becomes her emblem, as the *aegis*, symbol of ultimate protection, suggests Perseus is a channel between the two divinities, allowing the later to appropriate the earlier's meaning (much as Uatchet was absorbed by Isis) and ushering in a modern culture. When Siegfried killed the serpent-dragon Fafner and ate its heart and blood, the snake provided the hero, as the solar gods before him, with an expanded world. As Uncegila's heart had done, Fafner's meat released Siegfried from the mundane and brought his consciousness into super-nature by making him telepathic and privy to animal language. In both cases, through the snake, the hero enters a richer plane, either as go-between from culture to culture (Perseus) or as other-worldly communicator (Siegfried).

The Greek demi-divine Hercules (known as Ophioctonus or 'serpent-killing') combined two worlds within himself as an

An 1860s engraving of the infant Hercules strangling snakes as a symbol for 'Young America' strangling 'rebellion' and 'sedition' after the American Civil War.

archaic snake deity who survived into Hellenistic times as a serpent-slayer hero. Jane Harrison points out that Hercules was originally the Agathos Daemon snake (life force) and gained acceptance in the Olympian pantheon only by 'sloughing off his serpent-nature'.[16] However, snakes remained integral to his identity. As a baby, he strangled two serpents sent to murder him. As an adult, he had sexual liaisons with snake women and fathered their children. He was required to kill the seven-headed serpent Hydra, the snake-wreathed dog of Hell, Cerberus, and Ladon, the serpent custodian of the magic Hesperides apples, found at the end of the world. Hercules, who repeatedly destroyed the great time animal, was himself a time hero whose twelve labours encompassed the seasons, whose descent into hell confused life with death and whose award of the Plant of Invulnerability muddied his mortal state. He is also a saviour figure seen as a harbinger to Jesus, in part because he died horrifically and was given a heavenly place. His name meant 'glory of Hera', as the Delphic oracle decreed that his fame arose from what Hera's persecutions caused him to do. However, their relationship (as the name suggests) is multi-faceted, a distortion of Goddess-consort and it structures the many Herculean myths. Carl Jung specifically equates Hercules' struggle with Hera as the one between the (driven/heroic) consciousness and the (chaotic/ophidian) unconscious. Mythologist Karl Kerényi concedes Hercules a more cunning status, arguing that he is the double of Hermes, the Greek divine messenger, psychopomp, and trickster god of communication who carried the snake-entwined caduceus (symbolizing unified polarity). Hermes, after whom the hermetic tradition was named, was romanized as Mercurius, who became, as mercury, a medieval symbol of alchemy's holy grail: the alloy or synthesis. Though snakes are not typically connected to the global trickster, it can be argued that the trickster carries cosmic serpentine qualities. This character is, like the serpent, the soul of joined opposites. More importantly, he perpetrates ambiguity and with it maintains universal balance by mingling disorder with order, the role always assigned the divine snake. There is even a significant reverberation with Hermes, courier and communicator, in the stories of Perseus (the dispatcher) and Siegfried (the transmitter) when each integrated with the serpent.

Through the combat myth the snake degenerated into associations with evil, negativity, sin, magic, guile and duplicity. In India it is still held that if a cobra is killed, the murderer's face will impress into its eyes and the cobra's mate will hunt the killer, no matter how far away. Leprosy is believed to come from the terrifying Russell's viper's breath. The Christians took up this meaning, trying to disassociate (and protect) themselves from the pagan snake. They satanized it, made explicit in Revelations as 'that old serpent, called the Devil', a creature that could be female (to further emphasize its corruption) or male. As the

A 16th-century American Adam and Eve with the Devil, portrayed as both snake and female.

intricate relationship between 'good' and 'evil' was reduced to simplistic formulas, 'snake' became a convenient vilification for anything outside the current hegemony.

The complications of the ancient snake-heroes' ophidian traits interwoven with the divine snake-villains that they defeat dissipated as their stories became more quantified. Finally, in some cases, such as in Christianity, the struggles disintegrate into concrete Manichean allegories where the hero, such as St George or Jesus, conquers the snake-shaped Devil, or a ninth-century St Patrick drives the bad snakes from Ireland. In these stories, the serpent body is discarded – its power too frightening to tap. This one-time death prevails and the ritual of the daily conflict is lost, taking with it the continuing renewal of creative–destructive energy that fulfils the universe, conceived as the cosmological engine thousands and thousands of years before. This loss persisted even in modern thought. Jung justified the combat myth gestalt as the conflict between the mind's conscious (read solar hero) and the 'paralyzing' unconscious (read chaos serpent) which he called 'Lamia' after the Greek avenger she-serpent who devoured children.[17] In ranking the combat myth as only opposition/triumph, Jung missed the deeper level of resurrection (versus simple destruction) and the implicit generative push seen in the serpentine Sakti or the Neolithic double-snake icon. Recognized or not, both Sakti's envelopment and the uroboric circumference imbue the combat's theme of swallowing as the hero's final peril (about to be eaten), Ra's rejuvenation (from the serpent's mouth), and Jesus' similar return (from the maw of hell). The Palaeolithic time snake is at the base of this idea. This winding serpentine line is a 'body', an integument around universal beingness and around a Heideggerian *dasein* (the quality of being alive), holding infinity and becoming together, and out of which springs the diachronic or the renewed.

The Greek hero Jason, reborn from the serpent's mouth, appears to a snake-draped Athene wearing the Medusa-head aegis.

Despite a diminished status after the rise of the combat myth, the 'bad' snake still appeared as a 'good' resurrector, catalyst and orchestrator of antinomies in innumerable anecdotes and tall tales about health, immortality, regeneration or salvation. It is also the channelling snake of contemporary religion. An added major character, as in the Delphic oracle, Sioux creation tale and the *Lambton Worm*, is the 'old woman,' usually an adviser or healer or a supernatural/divine woman (even Eve), a carry over of the Great Goddess.

THE ELIXIR OF LIFE

Even if the snake seems to be a foil, it is actually central to the search for the Elixir of Life. This search, prominent in serpent mythology, is traceable to the Palaeolithic because, as it was then, the later *élan vital* is often fabled as a plant or tree protected by a snake. This pairing of serpent (synergy) coiled around tree (stability) became, as it was with the Greeks, the life symbol.[18] The *élan vital* appears in the Babylonian *Epic of Gilgamesh*, written *c*. 2000–1600 BC, surreptitiously connected to the Queen of Heaven, Innana, through her avatar, the snake. The hero Gilgamesh, fearing for his own life as Innana's lover, rebuffed her advances and, when his friend Enkidu mysteriously died in consequence, Gilgamesh avidly sought the Plant of Immortality. He found it at the ocean's bottom but it was stolen by a snake and eaten. By taking everlasting life for itself and outfoxing Gilgamesh, the snake is the goddess Innana's surrogate. Campbell sees a direct line between the Babylonian Plant with its snake and the Old Testament serpent in the Tree of Life. But this line extends even further: into eternal redemption.

The Gnostics, a Christian movement of Egyptian, Persian, Judaeic and Greek influences, especially strong in the second century AD but with sects contemporary with Jesus, such as the Naassenes (*naas:* Hebrew for serpent), conceived Eden's inveigling snake as a catalyst because, in jarring Eve from the stasis of Paradise, it precipitated the Fall and thus Christianity's *raison d'être* – salvation. This snake plays a Hermetic trickster role because its interjection of disorder into the status quo activates/emancipates an otherwise useless potential, echoing Ra's restoration, Osiris' chthonic commencement and Sakti's awakening.

In Hinduism, the snake's vigour elicited another Immortal Elixir, also from the sea's floor. In the 'Churning of the Milky Ocean', the gods and demons surrounded a submerged mountain with the giant multi-headed serpent Vasuki and pulled him back and forth. The agitation forced up Surabhi (Mother of All Things) and the Elixir. Vishnu, disguised as an old woman, gave it to the gods. The African Malagasy also bound the Elixir with the snake. European folklore is replete with similar pairings. In the eighteenth-century French story *Green Snake* (another

Beauty and the Beast), the heroine discovered that her invisible royal husband was a giant serpent. For years, she penitently tried to break his enchantment and finally, instructed by a fairy woman, went to the world's end for the Essence of Long Life. Down a deep (snake) hole, she found both it and her freed lover. In the German *The Three Snake Leaves*, snake and plant combine to resurrect. A serpent revived a mutilated, dead snake with leaves pressed to the cuts. A husband then did the same for his dead wife but she killed him. The leaves resuscitated him and she was executed. Albanian superstition holds that one snake can resurrect another, a belief echoed by contemporary Appalachian serpent handlers who, as we will see, testify that as holy channels they can raise the dead.

With thousands of years and a few continents separating them, these seemingly small, semi-secular tales have the same themes. The snake, as always, is proxy for immortality, reformation, resurrection and prosperity. It gains or maintains it as in the Babylonian story; causes it, as in the Hindu and Germanic lore; is privy to its secret, as in the Malagasy myth; or guards it, as in the French and Gnostic tales. The Elixir is found in geographic extremes, the ocean's floor or the world's end, the places where solar heroes Indra, Apollo and Jesus went to expiate their sins, and a woman is often the retriever or recipient.

SNAKE AND STAFF

A snake wound on a wand is a synecdoche of the Daimon and Tree and mirrors the spine or penis invigorated by Kundalini energy. The grasp of a wand, sceptre, crozier, crook or even a rolling pin signifies power and it has been speculated that the short Palaeolithic calendar sticks, which fall into this category, may be the prototype of the staff symbol.[19] The wand, the condensed universal body of transfiguration, is also a stiffened serpent, a shaft channelling the hand into what the wand touches.

Such wands are still actively relevant, some as staffs of sovereignty, such as the Senegalese snake staff, others as medical insignias. The wand of Asclepius, Greek god of medicine, with its single snake spiralling up a short stick, emblazons Western ambulances, hospitals, and pharmacies though few know what the sign means. The archaic holy snake incarnation, Asclepius, is a complex figure – god, saviour-healer, and hero-daimon – whom Jane Harrison likens to Zeus and to Hercules.[20] He was so influential (even into the Middle Ages) that Livy records that the Delphic oracle pronounced that a snake from his temple would end a Roman plague. The Hermetic caduceus, a winged staff entwined with two snakes, represents the living force spiralling around cosmic stability and showing (just as in the Neolithic) opposition as a unit, conjoining sickness and health, poison and healing. This displays the principle of immunity – extracting an antidote from what destroys. The snake was the prophylactic against death. Romans wore serpent rings as amulets (snake wrapped on staff-like finger). Hygeia, Roman goddess of health, always held a snake.

BEINGS AND INCARNATIONS

The snake being is a devolution of the serpent-wrapped Snake Goddess but even in this seemingly minor creature the supernal snake lives on in the harmony of opposites, tapping of sexual force and initiation of redemption. The snake as a half-human is really one thing: an adjudicator of unity and disunity. Even if malevolent, its purpose is to right whatever has gone wrong, however violently, and sexuality (the snake's creation aspect) is the place most used to enact this. The snake being is a shape-

A Renaissance
snake-tailed being,
from a 1650s
Italian book,
Vipera pythia.

shifter, appearing, like Green Snake, as both human and serpent. It combines a human body with a snake's skin, substitutes
a tail for legs, arms or hair, wears live snakes as belt, crown, jewellery, clothing, or resides inside a serpent. Snake tails, heads,
horns, locks or legs are also bestial attributes, from goats to cen-
taurs, made to instil fear or convey a chthonic or transcendent
purpose. Snakes combined with animals, elements or objects
express meanings such as immortality (with the stag), eternity
(with water) or renewal (with vases). Faces can spew snakes
from mouth, ears or eyes (as is typical in medieval Europe) or
have them slide on the skin (common in Africa, especially in
sixteenth-century Nigerian Benin imagery) to represent force,
life or command.

The serpent being is contradictory. It is frightful as the
Amerindian Kwakiutl Sisiutl, whose human head is set between
two serpent ones and who portends disaster. It is munificent
as the Chinese serpent-tailed Fu-Xi and Niu-kua, the fourth-

An Amerindian Kwakiutl divinity, Sisiult, who brings bad fortune, represented by one of the main dancers in the Winter Dance ceremonies, wearing a double-headed serpent mask and shirt made of hemlock bough, 1914, photograph by Edward S. Curtis.

millennium regal couple who founded civilization. Much as the Dogon origin serpent spat out the stones of binding social institutions, Fu-Xi and Niu-kua introduced all governing principles, especially those of matrimony, counting and the *I Ching* trigrams. Niu-Kua (as Jyoka) is credited with making humankind from mud into which she breathed life, as Yahweh did with Adam.

The most enduring snake beings are the Nagas (snakes) of Buddhism and Hinduism. Hindus retain cobra worship and its pre-Vedic heritage is visible in India's aboriginal Naga tribe, which still upholds women's rights and practices matrilinear heritage. The Nagas guard the cardinal points and control wind, tide, pestilence and drought. They are 'asuras', present instincts that fog the mind and deter self-realization. Yet, as children of the archaic Kadru ('Chalice of Immortality'), mother of the 'Ever-Moving' or the universal continuum, the Nagas are the everlasting cycles of time and the future's clarity. Their king,

Remainder, holds the residue of the universe in its billions of years of entropy. India, China, Thailand, Tibet, Cambodia and Japan show them as serpent-crowned humans or as snake-legged people but they can be depicted as snakes with human characteristics, living in the sea or underground in bedizened palaces. They understand birds (a talent that they instil in humans), hoard riches and knowledge, marry people and resurrect them. The warrior Arjuna (or Nagarjuna – Arjuna of the Serpents), the hero of the *Mahabharata*, married Ulupi, whose brother Vasuki (the snake who churned the ocean for the Elixir) possessed a 'jewel that grants all desires' and, when Arjuna died, this jewel revived him.

Muchalinda Naga, the Buddhist Serpent King, shielded the meditating Buddha (under the serpent's Tree) throughout his universal awakening. Muchalinda emerged from his hole, wrapped around the Buddha and covered him with his open cobra hood. On the last day, the snake became an obeisant man. Hans Zimmer sees in Muchalinda-Buddha the 'perfect reconciliation of antagonistic principles'.[21] They are a unit: Muchalinda, the dynamic, incarnates the birth–rebirth cycle and Buddha, the saviour, makes the snake the working foundation from which new transcendence springs: salvation (Buddha) is grounded in the universal grist (Muchalinda).

Sex is a serpent being strong suit. Stories are profuse with humans copulating with or marrying snakes. Snake-shifters figure largely in Amerindian mythology often in marriages that are frighteningly out of kilter where a woman, particularly, is tricked into wedding a serpent-human and, through ingenuity, finally gets away. These tales appear in Europe as the *Lindham Worm*, *Mesulina* or *Green Snake,* repeating similar patterns of a person loving someone bewitched, of a set condition, which is broken, and of lovers parted forever or, after tribulation, reunited. Some warn of demonic troubles and include murder and rape. The former tales begin with a husband or wife snake who, after hardships for both spouses, becomes human. Their union is truly right. The latter begin with a seductive man or woman who becomes a snake, usually treacherous. Their union is truly wrong. Even in these stories, the snake remains the transforming corpus wherein true unity is resolved and false unity exposed (as is so well expressed in the Dogon tale of the divine skirt).

Some marriages end in disaster. North American myths recount snakes biting women's vaginas and causing menstruation and women raped by snakes. Others are about disastrous partnerships, the converse of the pairing that breaks the tormenting spell. In the Chinese *Tale of the White Snake,* a fairy story much enacted in operas, plays and puppetry, a giant white snake transforms into a woman and marries. The couple lives contentedly but when a son is born, the wife regresses to snake form, eats the baby and kills her husband. In other versions, the child doesn't die and becomes a celebrated scholar. A Cambodian tale about a serpent goddess of the great temple Angkor Wat echoes the channelling serpent and the Meter-Attis relationship. The goddess slept nightly with the king but when she didn't appear, he was killed and a new king chosen.

The snake being also appears as a signature. The archaic European Daemonic snake, in late antiquity, became iconic, a shorthand for sanctity. Most Greek deities, such as Athene, Demeter, Hera, Hermes, Apollo and even Zeus[22] took serpent qualities as a means to anoint themselves with the holiness of their distant ophidian predecessor. This endorsement resurfaced in medieval alchemy when the uroboros acted as the perfect mystic synthesis.

The Medusa head, embossed onto Athene's shield, illustrates the shift from deity to symbol. The truth of the serpent-

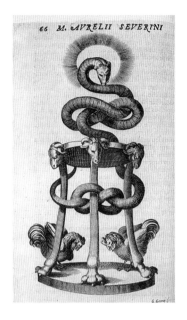

66 M. AURELII SEVERINI

An alchemical
snake, coiled in
mystic knots, from
a 1650s Italian
book, *Vipera
pythia*.

haired Medusa's status, as pure power, has been deformed in
history. The myth has it that the third of the three Gorgon sisters,
Medusa, whose stare turned all to stone, lived at the ends of the
earth. Perseus, thwarting her death ray by looking only at reflec-
tions, cut off her head and gave it to Athene who honored it as
the consummate *aegis*. This indicates the true nature of
Medusa's head. A primeval icon, always disembodied (the body
was added later), it is the Gorgon mask with glaring eyes, tusks
and fully extended tongue. This image is legion, traceable from
the Sioux Uncegila around the world to the Ethiopian Mensa
Bet-Abrahe's *heway*, a big, white serpent with a murderous look.
The Greek story essentializes the severing because *only* the head
is important: its purpose to carry the 'evil eye', able to inflict or
deflect terror. When given to Athene, Medusa's snaky visage

Gorgon head from a black-figure Greek vase painting.

returns to its rightful apotropaic role. Just as the Uatcheti became the uraeus on the divine Egyptian crown, the Medusa became the *aegis* on the divine Greek shield, signifying that its past was great. Neuman, emphasizing the dualism, suggests that Medusa is a polar serpent figure whose petrifying stare contrasts the cosmic serpent's vitalizing mobility. Medusa is life's rigid aspect, its rigor mortis, death. This echoes the Vedic Ananta whose body holds the 'dead' Vishnu as he sleeps.

The ophidian shorthand also encompassed the law. The snake's body, which once transformed the old regime into new, also ordained the transit of one custom into its successor. This is plainly exemplified by Aeschylus' fifth-century BC trilogy, *The Oresteia*, which, under its *grand guignol*, inscribes a cultural revolution. The story is of King Agamemnon's murder by his wife, Clytemnestra (in revenge for sacrificing their daughter), her murder by their son, Orestes (avenging his father), the wrath of the Erinyes or 'Angry Ones' (spirits who avenge matricide) upon him and his subsequent trial. The play establishes precedent by exonerating Orestes; Apollo nullifies his matricide, declaring that true birth is through the father, thus exulting patristic law over the previous matristic one.

However, the play is lined with ancient holdovers. Though Heracleitus calls the Erinyes 'ministers of justice' underscoring that, by his era, they literally *were* the Law, according to Jane Harrison, 'deep, very deep in the Greek mind lay the notion that the Erinyes . . . was a snake'[23] and Aeschylus associates them with their Medusa heritage:

> . . . they come like gorgons,
> they wear black robes,
> and they are wreathed in a tangle of snakes.

This association reaches further when the murdered Clytemnestra spurs the Erinyes to their 'deadly anger of the mother-snake' (Snake Goddess)[24] and Harrison argues that this connection is an almost 'unconscious slip' by Aeschylus.[25] Though on the cusp of a social modernity, he could not let go of his traditional belief that the divine serpent controlled all chthonic drama. The resurrecting snake is submerged in this play. Orestes should have died for his sin but, in the law's transformation through the serpentine Erinyes, he is saved. Their terrible justice mirrors the expiation paid by Apollo and Indra. In killing the creatrix of the world, these gods committed matricide and they paid as heavily as any Greek murderer, escaping death only through their divinity and a brutal penance.

Serpent beings are also allegorical. The common medieval bestiary, Christian propaganda set in natural history, is a good example of the ancient sacrosanct rendered into a metaphor. England's thirteenth-century *East Midlands Bestiary*, translated from the Latin two hundred years before, probably came from second-century AD Alexandria. Its 'Allegory of the Snake' has direct ties to the old serpent. The story describes an adder who deflects death by fasting until its skin loosens and, though weak, forcing itself through a stone's narrow hole to scrape the skin away. It then spews its venom and drinks water until 'revivified'. Like the dying snake, the Christian is 'wizened' without religious law and thus barred from heaven. But, the bestiary urges, if he becomes virtuous, he can squeeze through the 'hole of Christ', shed his wickedness and drink the gospel's holy water. Then he will become 'young and fresh' and the Devil will flee him. The sinner snake entering the 'hole in the stone' to relieve itself of sin conjures the simulated coitus of the Bacchic Mysteries, which purifies the initiate, and the snake's sin-and-sinless combination evokes Orestes' dual role (as condemned/exonerated) and the dyadic nature of all symbolic serpents.

DIVINE SAVIOUR

This same agency, once implicit within the Snake Goddess as the channelling snake who crossed from mundane to divine, living to afterlife, and lower to high plane, became increasingly reified into a saviour figure as diverse as the Egyptian Osiris (activated by the snake), Mayan Kulkulcan, Aztec Quetzlcoatl and Christian Jesus Christ.

Quetzlcoatl was clearly Messianic (he died, descended to the underworld and rose again) but his precursor, Kulkulcan, was an abstract 'deliverer' in one of the world's most fascinating metaphysical systems. For the Maya, Minoan contemporaries whose end came almost four thousand years later with the sixteenth-century Spanish conquest, Kulkulcan personified the Vision Serpent, revered as an energized access between divinely

Mayan stone serpent's head, Chichen Itza, Yucatan, Mexico.

inspired kings and the Otherworld and through whose body the king travelled to meet his ancestors and his gods. The serpent appears in many images but the Vision Serpent was paramount. Archaeologist Linda Schele notes that it and the double-headed Serpent Bar, a stylization of it, were the 'most profound symbols' of Maya kingship and that the existence of a shamanistic channel between worlds, incarnated by the snake, was the culture's core belief.[26] This belief dovetails with the Malian Dogon concepts, which took the serpent form to be a passage into an ordered existence. The Vision Serpent's mystic body, fortified by royal blood, was evoked in a cutting ritual. In this ceremony, the king or queen would pierce their own tongues and pass a rope embedded with thorns through the hole, catching blood drops on sections of paper. This painful, bloody act opened the way between the Mayan world's three co-existent layers: heaven, earth and underworld. All three, equally sentient, were linked by the axis of *wacah chan*, the World Tree. On its tip sat the celestial bird, and in its midst lay the Serpent Bar branches. As the royals cut themselves, a portal would be made and entered through the axis, which was ever-present and everywhere, and the World Tree would transform into the Vision Serpent through whose body the king, queen and their ancestors would travel. Along this mystic route, which encompassed a quantum sense of reality, every dimension was explored: past, present and future, death, life and immortality could be accessed without barrier. Mayan architecture reflected this channel because the portal of Xibalba, the underworld, was thought to be a giant serpent mouth. To mirror this, sacred caves, temples and houses were decorated with the same monstrous maw because it was believed that, as in the three world layers, all things reverberated into one another. In later centuries, the Vision Serpent lost its mutability and became a permanent symbol of the 'divinity of the state' in the figures of Kulkulkan or Queztlcoaltl.[27] The round smoking mirror, inset with four feathered snakeheads, was the prime icon of this change.

Even among Jews and Christians, so instrumental in demonizing the ophidion, the serpent contained strong traces of resurrection and wisdom. Moses, the Old Testament prophet, though not a redeemer, held a strange place between the pagan world and the Christian. He and his brother Aaron (with his

wand-snake)[28] are interpreted as possible snake shamans of Egyptian influence because of their un-Judaeic wielding of serpent power. During the Israelite exodus from Egypt, their god Yahweh sent vipers to punish non-believers and, after many fatalities, instructed Moses to make a bronze serpent draped on a pole. The snake, the means to spiritual and physical purification, was redemptive, curing anyone of snakebite who looked at it. The totem was worshipped, as Nehushtan, for centuries until destroyed as idolatrous. This mysterious symbol reappeared in the New Testament when Jesus claimed Moses' snake as a harbinger of his own coming. According to Tertullian, early Christians dubbed Jesus 'the Good Serpent' because he likened himself to this snake of atonement, saying 'as Moses lifted up the serpent in the wilderness, so must the Son of Man be lifted

Moses makes a bronze snake of redemption. An engraving of Gustave Doré's painting *The Brazen Serpent* (1883).

The Gnostic Jesus depicted as the crucified redeemer snake, from a 16th-century manuscript.

up; that whosoever believeth in him may have eternal life' (John 3:15). Matthew's instruction to '[b]e ye therefore wise as serpents, and harmless as doves' (Matthew 10:16) is even more explicit in the Gnostic Gospel of Thomas when Jesus makes the wise snake a portal to heaven:

> The Pharisees and the Scribes have received the keys of Knowledge, they have hidden them. They did not enter, and they did not let those enter who wished. But you, become wise as serpents and innocent as doves.

The Gnostics extended this. Viewing Yahweh as a vengeful 'demi-urge,' fearful of humankind's access to *gnosis* (knowledge), and the Edenic snake as his Christian usurper, they depicted Jesus as a serpent nailed to the cross. The Ophites (from the Greek *ophis* or serpent) even worshipped the snake and included a live one in their Eucharist with which they blessed their bread and then kissed on the mouth. With this rite, the snake corpus and Messianic corpus synergistically meld into a single sacerdotal agency as it had been doing for millennia. This conduit snake, so vital in Greek, African, Mayan, Judaeic, Christian and Gnostic belief, is still active. Today's snake-handling religions continue to treat the living snake as a real avatar and there are even degraded fragments of this belief in pornography and snake charming.

A snake charmer feeding the king's snakes, Dahomey, 1880s.

Serpent handling is an old business, existing for prurience, entertainment or worship, each probably a reflection of the other. The contemporary allure of women dancing with snakes, of charmers luring them or of believers holding them may be a distortion or continuation of ancient rites. But each has its own distinctions.

Sexualized serpent handling is mostly an exercise in erotic imagination but it has branches of violence and symbolism. At its most virulent, it is sadistically pornographic where snakes become dildos as women forcibly insert them in their vaginas. (In 2004, an American priest was accused of satanically using snakes in this way.) At its most benign, sexual serpent handling is sheer popism, with a history of lascivious prejudice and a current revival among stars such as Britney Spears (discussed in Chapter 6).

Lying somewhere between the sexual and the ceremonial is entertainment where snake handling has lost inherent meaning. Snake charming, an ancient art still practiced in Asia and Africa and often controlled by generations of one family, is its most obvious demonstration. Taking care not to frighten the animal, the charmer coaxes a snake from a basket not by music (it being deaf) but by a swaying body or object. The usual accusation is that poisonous snakes have been de-fanged or de-venomed. Some charmers, as in West Africa, are thought to rub their snakes with a herbal pulp that immobilizes their jaws and makes them dozy.

But of the three, the most enduring and perhaps most confounding, is sacred serpent handling, no doubt as old as religion itself. It probably impassioned Palaeolithic ceremonies, as Marshack argues, and certainly was central to ancient faith. Its

traces remain thematic in some beliefs but in others are real. Shamans who metamorphose into serpent familiars will mime the S-line as the means of transfiguration. It can be similarly sanctified in dance. The Cherokee, Creek, Yuchi, Seminole, Iroquoi, Winnebago, Sauk and Fox all have dances simulating a winding snake. Newly married West African women perform a python dance to ensure fertility. In antiquity, holy personages were tantamount to snake handlers. The Akkadian word for priest meant 'snake charmer' and Herodotus and Iamblichus reported that Egyptian priests called asps out of the altar of Isis. But its most dramatic form is still, after thousands of years, in

Indian charmers with snakes, c. 1890s.

A Louisiana
sideshow artist
eating a live
snake, 1938.

A dervish in
Kurdistan places
the head of a
poisonous snake
in his mouth,
1990.

the drastically effective wearing of snakes and in services where live serpent handling is essential, such as those of the American Holiness Church and the Hopi Indian.

Serpents are usually worn as a warning. Some people drape themselves with them as did the Psylli (ancient African snake hunters), or as do Thai snake charmer women who whirl intrepidly with snakes' heads in their mouths. But the most striking is snake attire of a divine being. Since the serpent indicated the chthonic and supernal, female deities typically were adorned in them. Greek goddesses such as Athene, Artemis, Hecate and Persephone as well as the Erinyes and the high priestesses of Delphi and Crete held snakes, wore them or were guarded by them. The Gorgon Medusa was often painted with a belt of living snakes, as were the mad Bacchantes. The Celtic goddesses Danu (water, wisdom, magic) and Epona (horses, agriculture)

Snake-draped celebrants at a Caribbean carnival held at Port au Prince in Haiti, 2004.

were wreathed in snakes and Brighit or Bride (hearth, science,
culture) who was romanized by the Celts as Minerva and chris-
tianized as St Bridget wore a waistband of snakes. As late as the
nineteenth century, a prayer about taming serpents was made
to her.

But some snake-draped deities were particularly gruesome. The Great Goddess, especially in later incarnations, often appeared as a triumvirate of creator-preserver-destroyer and the serpent communicated her destruction. The Babylonian demon Lamashtu, a female with taloned feet and lioness head, held long serpents in each hand. The terrifying Aztec Coatlicue, Lady of the Skirt of Serpents, dressed in snakes. A primal Earth Mother, she was birth/death, filth/redemption (she ate the filth of sin to offer redemption), and Heaven/Hell. Her necklace of human hands, hearts and skulls hung around her neck, where two blood streams, shaped as snakes, issued in lieu of a head. Her feet and hands were claws. The Aztec Cihuacoatl, Serpent Woman, originator of humanity and goddess of childbirth, was shown encased within a snake, her face peering from the open mouth.

The most famous snake-hung deity is the terrible Hindu triumvirate Kali (Primordial Abyss, World Mother and Destroyer), a pre-Vedic goddess who ruled with Śiva (also Shiva) before the Aryan invasions. Like Kundalini, she probably evolved from the Dravidian Snake Goddess whose naked human figure was depicted upside down with spread legs and a plant blooming from her vulva and whose piled hair was a coil of snakes. This coif represented 'serpent' and any person wearing the style did so as a symbol of omniscience. Kali is a time divinity. Her black skin is the essential nothingness from which all creation comes and into which it goes. She drips blood to show death (bleeding) and life (menstruation). As Primordial Abyss, she is the universal womb. As World Mother, she fosters each generation. As Destroyer, she is life's degradation and her tongue hangs out, her clothes bleed and she is slung with live cobras. Śiva (who has no power without Kundalini), on whose body Destroyer Kali dances, is often circled with snakes around his neck or penis to underscore his relationship with time serpent Sakti.

Today, live snakes still represent holiness for faiths as diverse as Voodoo, Hopi spiritualism and Pentecostal Christianity. Voodoo, as a derivative of North and West African religion where the python is venerated as water/fertility, has dominant serpent motifs. Dan Petro, the Rainbow Serpent, and Simbi, serpent god of water and magicians, are implied in some snake handling of Haitian Voodoo. Obeah priestesses in Dutch Guiana had giant snakes, called amodites or papa, follow them at will and ordained West Indian women were reported by nineteenth-century Europeans to simulate intercourse using live snakes. (This is apocryphal and probably about the Bamboule, a worker's dance celebrated throughout the Caribbean and Louisiana, but still has credence among those who like the idea.) Serpentine movements embroider Voodoo ritual and a Haitian priest can mimic the snake's coiling so well that he seems transformed.

But the Hopi Indians have an intimate relationship with the live snake and respect it as an avatar. They believe that dead sorcerers return as bull snakes, which, if killed, will free the soul. The Snake Clan conducts the ancient Snake Dance, an annual nine-day ceremony to induce rain, held in Arizona and New Mexico. Much of the event is secret but four days are spent hunting a rattlesnake species known as *nuntius*, meaning 'messenger' (one hundred can be caught). On the last day at sundown, after a washing rite, the priests, dressed as mythic figures, slowly dance in a ring, carrying live snakes in their mouths and replacing them periodically. After many hours, the priests run down the mesas into sacred areas where the snakes are freed to take messages to the gods. There have been few reports of bites but one outside observer claimed that the

A Hopi priest during the annual Snake Dance, Phoenix, Arizona, c. 1899.

A Holiness Church believer with a snake, Kentucky, 1946.

snakes have had their fangs (*and* their replacement fangs) extracted.

The American Holiness Church of Signs Following, a derivative of Christian Charismatic Pentecostalism, also handles lethal snakes. Despite outlawing in some states, this denomination is not uncommon along the Southern belt. The movement arose from a literal interpretation of the biblical line – 'and they shall take up serpents' (Mark 16). The passage demands that the true believer perform five tasks: cast out devils, speak in tongues, take up serpents, drink deadly substances, and cure the sick. The snake, though considered by the Signs Following as the Devil's tool, nevertheless retains its qualities as channel (to Jesus), healer (raising the sick), communicator (speaking in tongues), defier of death (drinking deadly liquids) and purifier (casting out devils).

The groups have various names but all follow a similar format. Women and men participate and children attend. Most adults witness, handle two or more serpents in their ecstatic 'anointed' states, and sometimes drink poison. The services are excited, with shouting, praying, babbling and music. The women, who tightly bind their hair, loosen it while holding snakes. Part of the church for generations, devotees believe that their faith is a true connection to another world. One awestruck woman testified that '[w]e believe you can raise the dead'.[29] There have been troubles. The Signs Following never defangs, milks or drugs a snake and numerous people have been bitten and some have died. In 1991, a scandal rocked the community when a veteran preacher, who attempted to murder his wife by snakebite, was sentenced to life imprisonment. The participants are by and large white, poor and rural and many have expressed an unprecedented sense of power and transcendence in their lives when they handle snakes. But to reduce the experience to poverty is to miss the potency of the belief. It's not far-fetched to see thousands and thousands of years of serpent worship, across the world, in a room of entranced faithful. The tiny wooden church in Tennessee could be a torch-lit cavern of Bacchic worshippers in Greece where an initiate thrills to the god's avatar snake, a sunlit plaza of Chichen Itza where a Mayan king slices his tongue to call up the Vision Serpent, a stepped Hindu altar where the believer feels the presence of a snake-bedaubed Kali, a hot, hilltop shrine where a Minoan priestess raises a snake in each hand, a dry incense-filled stone temple where a goddess in serpent form is drawn from a crack by an Egyptian hierophant, or the faintly lit, painted underground cave where Palaeolithic hands first gave life to the snake divinity. Holiness Church Barbara Elkins's words may purposefully speak for all:

> I would never consider giving up serpent handling. No. Never. There is no way you can take hold of the reins and then look back. Now, I want more of the Lord.[30]

3 Venomous Snake

The snake's roles as catalyst and unifier are mirrored in its most astounding biological quality: venom, one of nature's truly unusual substances.

Snake venom terrifies. Its havoc is so enormous, literally and psychologically, that it throws light on the question of why snakes were singled out for extreme symbolism. Yet out of some 2,600 species, only just over a quarter are deadly. They can be found in the ocean (the killer sea kraits of South East Asia), in trees (the African boomslang), in jungle swamps (the Asian king cobra), in mountains (the American rattlesnake) or underground (the Middle Eastern burrowing asp). These 600 groups belong to one superfamily, the Xenophidia Colubroidea, emerging some 40 million years ago, which has four major sub-families – Viperidae, Colubridae, Atractaspididae, Elapidae – by no means all of which are lethal.

The venomous snake is the most advanced of the species. Streamlined and agile, with sharp delicate teeth, and no vestigial limbs, it gained superiority over its non-lethal cousins primarily because its venom enhanced its survival. The venomous snake can kill a large animal and quickly break down its body once swallowed. This gives it great advantage over those, from the giant anaconda to the little garden snake, that must subdue prey with strength, face harm in the fight and be encumbered

The lithe, deadly sea krait, from Patrick Russell's 1790s *Account of Indian Serpents*.

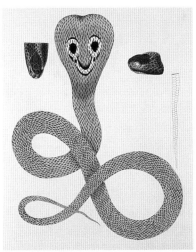

The 'eyeglass' markings on the cobra's hood, from Patrick Russell's *Account of Indian Serpents*.

by a long digestion. But the venomous snake suffers its own drawbacks. It feels aridity and cold more than constrictors, is less fertile and has weaker camouflage.

Snake venom (and reptile venom in general) is among the most biologically complex, and most enigmatic, of natural properties. André Ménez, director of Protein Chemistry at the Commissariat à l'Energie Atomique in France, describes venom as a 'remarkable factory'[1] because it both creates and destroys so much. Science has been slow to understand its make-up and even in the 1950s no one was sure how to classify it. It was thought that snake venom simply paralyzed and international studies through the 1960s supported this. But once its proteins were isolated in the 1970s, the intricacy of its chemistry began to be revealed.

Its function and composition have always fascinated science and for good reason. Venom's ability to cause extreme physical consequences, from haemorrhaging to sweating to delirium, makes it a source of anything from murder to revelation to cure. Venom can induce a potent, albeit risky, high and is now argued to be the cause behind some hallucinatory, occult or prophetic perceptions. The Sioux believed that if a young, dancing man was bitten by a snake and didn't die, he would experience a universal awakening. (Since ancient times, dancing was felt to be an ecstatic mimesis of the mystical and is still seen as the means by which mysteries are disclosed.)[2] Snake venom was lapped to induce trances at Delphi. Even some scientists testify to experiencing altered states from snakebite, seeing visions and feeling enormous capabilities. Venom has been used in medicine from ancient times as a relief for problems as diverse as melancholy, cough, eczema, impotence and the plague. These ideas are still active in both Eastern and Western healing. Across Asia, the snake is considered a potent physic. As a yin principle, it

warms, boosts, stimulates and is an ingredient in many remedies, especially as a jolt to the circulation or the immune system. A widely favoured general tonic, found in any Chinese
pharmacy, is that of a snake's gall bladder (particularly the copperhead, grass snake and black-ringed krait), distilled in alcohol, which is sipped daily. Western medicine is casting a wider
net. Crucial new breakthroughs around diseases as deadly as
Alzheimer's, stroke and breast cancer are happening as science
is tapping into the phenomenon of venom.

What is snakebite really? Snakebite, depending on its
toxin, will cause a variety of reactions, usually incremental.
These can be pain, dizziness, tingling, difficulty breathing,
shock, vertigo, bleeding, sweating, drooling, chills, tunnel or
blurred vision, nausea, tenderness, bruising, blistering,
swelling until the skin splits open, blackening of the flesh as
the tissue dies, seizure, sleepiness, coma, paralysis, haemorrhage, gangrene, decreased blood pressure, heart attack and, in
some cases, lockjaw, loss of an appendage, scarring, permanent
nerve damage or death. Transfusions can require up to 1.5 litres
(3 pints) of blood.

Though snake venom is usually classified as a neurotoxin and
haemotoxin, all venoms contain elements of both and, though
it is a mistake to sort snakes into these black and white divisions,
each species carries more of one toxin over the other and thus is
categorized by what predominates. Neurotoxic venom blocks
the nerve receptors, devastating the nervous system. The victim
is paralyzed, the muscles stop working, breathing fails and disintegration sets in immediately. Colubridae and Elapidae found
throughout the world, including cobras, coral snakes, sea snakes
and kraits, have this type of toxin. Haemotoxic venom attacks
the blood, literally diluting it, causing haemorrhage by instilling
a compound that prevents clotting. The victim bleeds to death.

The North American *viperidaes* such as copperheads, rattlesnakes
and cottonmouths have this kind. Variables such as the size of
the victim or snake, the amount of venom used, the bite's depth
or even the air temperature (snakes make less venom during
winter), affect the efficacy of snakebite. A snake controls how
much venom it emits, often as little as 10 per cent. This varies
from species to species and even regionally. Restricting doses are
vital as it can take between two weeks to two months for venom
to replenish. Even with toxic serpents, 20 to 30 per cent of
people who have been bitten hard enough to show marks have
no venom in their blood because the snake has sprayed before
the strike.

The carrier of such biological violence is complex. Basically
a saliva, venom is thought to have evolved over millions of years
from simple, digestive juices since, though venom is a defence,
its properties of disintegration and paralysis exist to make swallowing and ingestion easier. All snakes are carnivorous but

they can't chew or tear. A snake is vulnerably limbless and mal-leable with no tusks or claws to restrain prey. Venom subdues the bitten animal and then swiftly corrupts its flesh. The body becomes a pulpy mass as its organs and muscles collapse or as it floods with blood. Venom also increases absorption, prevent-ing the corpse from rotting in the stomach and saving the snake from poisoning.

A clear, dark or light yellow viscous liquid, venom is made up of a host of enzymes, of which 90 per cent are proteins. An enzyme propels biological action (echoing the symbolic serpent as instant generator of pure life). Venom's primary purpose is to destroy tissue and rush toxin into the body. Twenty-five sepa-rate enzymes have been found in snake venoms throughout the world. All snakes share ten of these and the rest are mixed, in varying proportions, within the venom of each species. Part of the venom's complexity lies in the snake's venom gland, which is designed to isolate proteins and toxins. The gland 'wraps' each separately until an unknown mechanism binds them and

The poisonous beadsnake coiling round a sweet potato.

they activate, rather like mixing two glue components together to activate its adhesive properties. The mythic consolidator of opposites has a biological base.

Venom sits in a long, oval-shaped gland between the eye and mouth, extending to the back of the skull (in most snakes; in some, like the South-East Asian long-glanded snake, it runs through half its body). A thin duct leads under the eye into the fangs, which are hollowed much like a hypodermic needle and through which the snake shoots its poison. The gland even differs between snake families. Colubrids have a 'Duvernoy' gland and viperids, elapids and sea snakes have a larger 'venom' gland. Both have an accessory gland encasing the fang's gum.

Fangs are periodically shed and replaced every few months (a hint of the tooth is always visible behind the one in use). Like venom, their evolution has effected the snake's survival, its diversification around the world, and its superiority. Dentition is a basic factor in snake classification. The primitive Aglyphous (Greek for 'without a groove') snake, like the blind snake and the boa, has uniform teeth and no fangs. As snake teeth evolved, they lost their weightiness, surface grooves folded inwards (in most snakes) and enclosed, transforming into hollow canals or what became the contemporary fang. This venom-ducted tooth is in the front or the back of the mouth. The rear-sited ones (sitting just beneath the eye) appear in the Opisthoglyphous ('groove at back') snakes. Until the mid-twentieth century herpetologists dismissed the deadliness of the rear-fanged snake, such as Africa's boomslang, but after obvious fatalities (two renowned scientists), its toxicity was recognized. As the venom gland developed, the front teeth narrowed. Proteroglyphous ('groove at front') snakes have short to long needle-like fangs, extending virtually below the nostril. All elapids fall into this category. The American coral snake fixes its short teeth into prey and, in a sense, chews, to infuse the venom. The long-fanged Indian cobra, conversely, will strike with amazing speed, stabbing in and pulling its teeth quickly out. Some fangs are fixed. Others are hinged, so that the teeth can lie against the jaw until muscles pull them forward for the strike position. The Solenoglyphous ('pipe' or 'groove') snakes, and all viperids, are the most highly adapted. They have two hinged front fangs, which, during a bite, spring out and lock. The mouth opens almost 170 degrees, allowing the strike to be quick and deep. This is typical in the American rattlesnake, African puff adder and India's saw-scaled viper, as well as in pit vipers, such as the Latin American terciopelo or fer-de-lance.

A venomous snake can move its fangs to attack in one-twentieth of a second. It can strike at 36 km/h (22 mph), so fast it can barely be filmed. The saw-scaled viper, cobra and lance-head cause most deaths. Some of the largest deadly snakes are the king cobra (at 3 to 5 metres or 10–16 ft long), asp, copper-head, rattlesnake, coral snake, cottonmouth, saw-scaled viper, mamba, Gaboon viper, death adder, puff adder, boomslang and terciopelo. The most venomous are the inland Taipan, the king cobra and the black mamba. The last, a slender, dully coloured snake found south of the African Sahara, has the world's most lethal toxin. Able to move at speeds of 14.5 km/h (9 mph), it can rear up fully two-thirds of its body and will strike in seconds and kill in minutes.

Though venom is hair-raising and its damage to flesh horrific, it has always been a secret weapon in medicine and, despite its use as a metaphor for illness or harm, can perform miraculous wonders. It can rush transformative destruction through the body, dissolve capillary walls, deteriorate red or white blood cells, alter and stop heart rhythms, prevent or cause blood clotting, block nerve impulses, freeze the diaphragm and interfere

Venomous snake
representing
tuberculosis, 1918
French litho-
graphic poster.

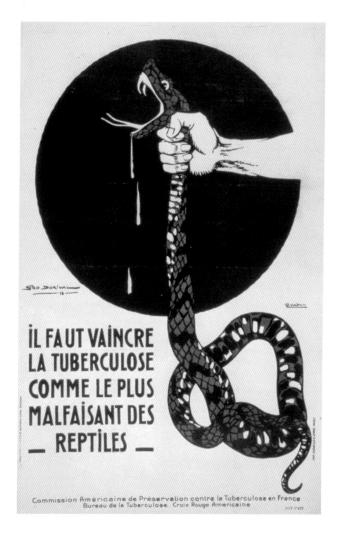

with brain waves. Because of these lightning processes, snake venom is being avidly researched in treatment for illnesses such as breast cancer, stroke, Parkinson's disease, heart attack, high blood pressure, angina, neuritis, thrombosis, epilepsy, cataracts, Lou Gehrig's disease, Alzheimer's, arthritis, rheumatism, and other killers such as malaria, hepatitis and botulism. It is an effective pain suppressant, anti-coagulant and coagulant. Sometimes, the same enzyme controls opposing states.

Venom's properties are studied in laboratories and universities around the world but the largest, state-of-the-art snake research centres are in Brazil, Tanzania and the United States. These breed snakes for venom or have them professionally caught. Processed snakes, out of anxiety or excess handling, produce more poison. Venom is sold to regular clients and there is a brisk trade in cobra, coral snake, sea krait and pit viper venoms, much of which can be bought through the Internet. Often some thousand plus snakes are kept in small boxes, in intensely monitored quarantine. Visitors are forbidden (as potentially contagious) and personnel are constantly cleansed.

Not only must a specific venom be linked to a specific illness, but venom's complicated make-up, subtly or drastically variant, means that only certain components are extracted. Venom-based products have not always worked, partly because of potential risks, and partly because the toxins are too complex for science to decode. However, drugs companies have lucratively marketed some medicines. In the 1930s, a New York doctor began working with spider poison for pain relief and moved to cobra venom, achieving a strong analgesic that was used for 20 years. More effective than morphine, it unfortunately produced double vision and stomach upset. By the 1960s, these experiments broadened. Researchers in Brazil isolated a peptide in jararaca venom, which eventually led to the manufacture of the highly successful hypertension drug with few side effects, Captopril. The enzyme fibrolas in copperhead venom, capable of clot dissolution, is being examined for stroke prevention, heart attack and similar cardiovascular illnesses. The protein contortrostatin from the same snake, also an anti-coagulant, is being developed as a potential cure for breast and ovarian cancer because it can bar a malignancy from entering the bloodstream. Since the early 1970s, cobra venom's cytotoxins, which can break down cells and hence could destroy tumours, have been part of general cancer research. Cobra venom is also being tested in research into multiple sclerosis and Parkinson's disease. Analgesics have long been developed from it. In China, cobra-based treatments such as Cobroxin, which stops nerve transmission, and Nyloxin, which reduces arthritic pain, are widespread. The highly toxic sea snake venom has some effect on memory loss and has become key to Alzheimer's research. Malayan pit vipers are being studied for stroke. An anti-coagulant, Arvin, has been extracted from their toxin.

Viper venom is especially good for promoting blood clotting and dissolving blood clots. The American company Merck, in the late 1990s, launched the powerful anti-clotting drug, Aggrastat, based on saw-scaled viper venom. Protac, a drug that corrects deficiencies leading to vascular thrombosis, has been developed from water moccasin venom. Batroxobin, an enzyme taken from lancehead venom, is used in the drug Reptilase. This component corrects flaws in a plasma protein, fibrinogen, which is essential to coagulation. The same enzyme (which cements clots) is used in Defibrase but as an opposite agent, one that dissolves clots. (Again, the mythic polar unification is made real within the serpent's body.) The common beta-blocker, used against cardiovascular disease, is rooted in venoms of snakes such as the terciopelo. In 2004, the beta-blocker

Propanolol was marketed as an active agent against memory loss.

Homoeopathy too treasures venom. In 1882, J. W. Hayward, a British homoeopath, produced a long treatise on the benefits of rattlesnake venom. It is still used, and venom in general makes up 2 per cent of all homoeopathic remedies, particularly those relating to the heart, circulation, pain and haemorrhage.

André Ménez argues that drug research has two future avenues: to continue to trailblaze new medications or that 'toxin-like compounds, mimicking those of venom, be designed for special targets'. The latter is still unfulfilled but he proposes that the structure of toxin, in time, may be applied to solutions for illnesses such as HIV.[3]

The snake and its venom weren't well examined until the seventeenth century. Ancient natural historians such as Aristotle and Pliny and those of the Middle Ages basically viewed the serpent through allegory and lore. By the sixteenth century, ideas about venom in Europe began to form but were still fanciful. Edward Topsell wrote *The Historie of Serpents* (1608), which, despite some accurate findings, was essentially a compendium of tales. But the same century saw the first substantial venom study. Jan Baptista van Helmont, the Belgian disciple of Paracelsus and a chemist of some repute, who first recognized distinct gases, argued that snake venoms were 'irritated spirits', so cold that they froze the blood to a paralyzing death. Francesco Redi, an Italian physician, overthrew these ideas through simple experimentation, deducing that venom was a lethal liquid emitted from the fang. But it was Felix Fontana, another Italian, who began to unravel the secrets of the apparatus. In 1781, though not able to differentiate one venom's action from another, his *Treatise on Viper Venom* recognized that venom congealed blood, a major finding in venom research. He also proved that the poison was not toxic if swallowed and that only blood contact counted. In the same era, the Swede Carolus Linnaeus devised the first true natural order of snakes, a work much refined over the next hundred years, which by 1854 included the vital dentition taxonomy. As chemistry developed, and the concept of 'protein' was isolated and named, the complex protein-rich venom increasingly fascinated scientists and experiments with specific venoms began. The first charting of venom's properties was drawn up in 1901. By the 1920s, the all-important distinction between its toxicity and its immunogen was discovered and substantial research into modern antivenin began.

Luckily for them, with proteins in their bloodstream that disarm poison, almost all snakes are immune to their own venom. For the rest of us, antivenin is needed. Like any vaccine, antivenin must be created from the substance it protects against. Venom is 'milked' from a snake when its fangs are forced into a covered glass until its toxin drips. Some snakes, such as cobras, are better milked by hand because more venom is yielded. Others, such as vipers and mambas, are best milked by electrodes, which, put to the snake's head, force muscle contractions and release poison. Freeze-dried, packaged and kept in the dark at -50°C (-58°F), venom can remain active for decades. (Even a taxidermied snake can still have deadly venom!) The powder (mixed with liquid) is injected into a horse whose blood plasma slowly builds antibodies, which form the serum's base. This type was first introduced in the USA in 1954 but, in the last ten years better serum has been derived from sheep's blood, which has less allergic risk. A polyvalent serum is nearly impossible to make. Serums are best matched to specific snakes or snake groups. In central Africa, for example, serums group around the green and the black

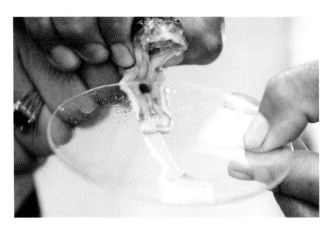
Milking a snake of its venom.

mamba, certain cobras and the puff adder. In Europe, antivenin is typically drawn from vipers such as the adder and the asp.

Approximately 125,000 people die annually of snakebite, one-fifth in the Americas and Africa combined and the rest in Asia. Snakes are fairly secretive and it can be harder to get bitten by one than to be hit by lightning, but there are countries where this isn't true. India, highly populated and very rural, bears the brunt of envenomation deaths. Twenty-five per cent of the world's bitten people die there, where the dreaded saw-scaled viper, one of the world's greatest killers, is indigenous. Antivenin is in demand and the country boasts some of the world's most skilful snake catchers. An interesting outgrowth of the ban on snakeskin, which became law in 1972, has been the Irula Cooperative. The Southern Indian Irula tribe, generations of snake catchers who once sold skins, were re-employed as snake catchers to gather and milk snakes.

Snake antidote has a curious history. Poisoning, from the Mediterranean to the Far East, was not an uncommon means of

An early 20th-century snake-bite kit.

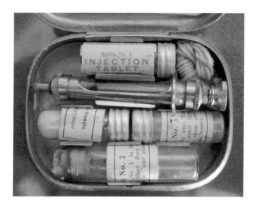

murder in the ancient world and fear of it was widespread. Even the Judaeic god Yahweh used poison as a revenge when he sent 'fiery serpents' against which 'there was no charm' (Numbers 21:5) to bite the complaining Israelites fleeing Egypt. People often took a generic antidote, sometimes daily, to protect themselves, effectively or not. Salesmen, known as 'charmers of the crowd', would hawk any kind of antivenin in the market place, and the Roman naturalist Pliny the Elder declared that a person would be insane to buy from them. Similar charlatans selling remedies showed up centuries later as 'snake-oil' salesmen.

The earliest known trade in venom and antivenin goes back to 1500 BC and was led by the Psylli, a North African Snake clan. Renowned for a natural immunity to snakebite, probably induced by frequent bites from immature snakes, the Psylli went so far as to expose their infants to snakes to prove this lineage. On finding a serpent, they would scream, foam at the mouth and rip the animal apart with their teeth. Highly revered, as they danced with snakes, people would touch them for their charmed strength. Their traditions continued well into the eighteenth century. Even Napoleon sent for a Psylli to evict a cobra when he was in Egypt. Other such famous ancient snake traders were the North African Nasamones and Palaeothebans, the Ophiozenes of Cyprus and the Marsi of Italy. Pliny described the Marsi as having, like the Psylli, a personal immunity, in this case, a quality inherited from their ancestor Circe, the sorceress who ensnared Odysseus. In the sixteenth century, a Pauline group, who tolerated snakebite like the Marsi, attributed their success to St Paul. The prophylactic serpent was used in France in the same era. At the court of Louis XIV, snake powder blended in olive oil was given as an antidote (ineffectually) to the (apparently) poisoned Duchess of Orléans.

The ancient Egyptians regarded snakebite as so serious they felt the soul of a bitten person was desecrated. Even a mummy took a snakebite amulet into the Underworld. In the first century AD, Greek physician Dioscorides extolled the virtues of the herb viper's bugloss against snakebite (or any poison) but warned that it must be eaten before the bite. Producing a heavy sweat as well as copious lactation, it forestalled two kinds of problems: the biological, such as a chill-inducing fever, and the psychological, such as melancholy. Another plant thought effective was the Latin American Virginian snake-root, which could supposedly dope a snake, a trick attributed to Egyptian snake handlers. Abscess root, a North American plant, was good for snakebite, skin disease and lung ailment. Spotted stones known as ophites or serpent marble were thought to cure snakebite and relieve headache. Lemon juice mixed with tamarind, and drunk from a rhino horn, has been used as a snakebite remedy allegedly, in part, because the ascorbic acid speeds healing. Celsus, the Roman writer, recorded a remedy used for thousands of years until discredited in the last decade. He suggested that the bitten person apply a tourniquet, that cuts be made near the wound and the blood sucked. This was also advocated by Moses

Maimonides, twelfth-century Rabbinic scholar and physician to Saladin, who treated leprosy and cancer with venom. (Now it is known that a bite should never be interfered with in any way. Methods such as sucking, tourniquets, ice packs or alcohol only cause further damage. Antivenin is the best remedy.) Stones like the Arab bezoar, a kind of stony accretion found chiefly in sheep's stomachs, were said to neutralize poison. The so-called snake stone, a charred cow's bone, through a weird rite was meant to draw venom from the wound. In the *Nag Panchami* festival, Indian villagers catch snakes and give them milk, hoping this will preclude any future fatality. But in case of a bite, the Garuda deity, said to be immune to snake poison, is sought and a bitten person will embrace a Garuda pillar. Senegalese snake handlers sell charms, called *gris-gris*, which ward off bites, and can be tied to the legs or arms. The Sudanese wear *hejab,* small leather cases full of amulets and Koran verses, as snakebite prevention. They draw a pentacle around a bite as an invocation to Solomon, Arabic ruler of the djinn and Judaeic ruler of demons (which can appear as snakes). The medical profession advocated electric shock as an antidote to snakebite in the late twentieth century, though it has never proved beneficial.

One of the earliest recorded snake antidotes appears in the third century BC and its strange international career lasted over 2,000 years, until the nineteenth century. Hannibal, the Carthaginian leader, wrought biological warfare on the Romans by hurling earthen jars filled with poisonous snakes at their ships. Breaking loose on the decks, the snakes bit the sailors who jumped into the sea. (Angry colonists suggested a similar tactic during the American Revolution by advocating the release of rattlesnakes in London's parks and private gardens.) The Greek Andromachus, physician to the Roman general Neron, on his instruction, sought a simple antivenin. In some versions, he doctored the emperor Nero, who requested a universal panacea. Both cures became attached to Andromachus' recipe of poisonous dried snake flesh and other ingredients, including opium, called 'theriake' (from the Greek, *the'riaka* meaning a drug [*pharmaka*] for a wild animal [*thr*] bite). The mixture became known as *Theriaca Andromachi*, a phrase soon bastardized into 'treacle'. The Roman version, an electuary paste, included 64 (or 73) drugs and spices mixed with honey. The uber-prophylactic reputation of 'treacle' travelled the world as a drug, remedy and metaphor, becoming *the* great poison antidote, able to subdue the most virulent foe, from the Devil to the plague, the plainest ulcer or the most elusive depression. By the twelfth century, Venice, now the main port for the burgeoning sugar trade, produced and supplied theriaca to most of Europe and 'treacle' became 'Venice treacle', or more rarely Orvietan, after the Italian town of Orvieto where it was first sold. What did it consist of?

Seventeenth-century herbalist Nicholas Culpeper, in his *The Compleat Herbal*, gives a full recipe for Venice treacle which includes 'troches of vipers', 'opium of Thebes', turpentine, myrrh, roses, cinnamon, liquorice, horehound, parsley, nutmegs, annis, roman vitriol, burnt saffron, fennel, carrot and Canary wine, mixed into a paste that is 75 per cent honey. Culpeper's remedy is explicit and far ranging. It

resists poison, and the bitings of venomous beasts, inveterate headaches, vertigo, deafness, the falling-sickness, astonishment, apoplexies, dulness of sight, want of voice, asthmaes, old and new coughs, such as spit or vomit blood, such as can hardly spit or breathe, coldness of the stomach, wind, the cholic, and illiac passion, the yellow jaundice, hardness of the spleen, stone in the

Plantain plant as snake-bite antidote from a 15th-century Italian *Herbarium*.

veins and bladder, difficulty of urine, ulcers in the bladder, fevers, dropsies, leprosies, it provokes the menses, brings forth birth and after-birth, helps pains in the joints, it helps not only the body, but also the mind, as vain fears, melancholy, &c. and is a good remedy in pestilential fevers.

Thomas Fuller's *Pharmacopoeia Extemporanea* (1710) focuses on venom's known properties in his Venice treacle description:

It dissolveth clotted Blood, and heals internal Wounds, provokes Sweat and Urine, is very good for Women after Labour, let those that have caught a Bruise, take it 3 times a Day after Bleeding.

The 1746 *London Pharmacopeia* also outlined its some 70 ingredients. Virtually two millennia after Andromachus concocted his theriaca, Venice treacle was a potion still much in demand.

During the Middle Ages, Venice treacle was the most widely
used cure-all, second only to leeches. *The Book of Theriaque,* a
twelfth-century Persian manuscript, relayed two stories regarding
the principle of theriaca's superpower. In both, the miracle
exists in venom's ability to excise venom. Not only is this a
property of antivenin but it shows the same dualism found in

Medusa's petrifying/protecting effect and the entwined universal Neolithic serpents that reappear on the caduceus. In one
story, a king's courtier, poisoned by an enemy, is then bitten by
a snake. The bite nullifies the first toxin and the man lives. In
the second, doctor Andromachus, now 'druggist' Andrimakhus,
sees a leper cured after drinking jugged wine containing a venomous snake. The Middle East version of theriaca, called tiryák,
was made with much the same treacle formula, and the best
came from Iraq.

Inevitably, treacle became symbolic for an invulnerable
defence. Culpeper described garlic as the 'poor man's treacle'. It
solidly entered Christian metaphors where the serpent was the
implied synecdoche for evil and Jesus the antivenin. Geoffrey
Chaucer smoothed the two together when he declared 'And
Christ that is unto all ills triacle'. Thomas More, Henry VIII's
intransigent Catholic chancellor, echoed this when he proposed
a 'most strong treacle against these venomous heresies'. The
Old Testament's 'balm' (Jeremiah 8:22) sought in the town of
Gilead was translated, in 1568, as a 'treacle'; the sixteenth-century edition is still known as the 'Treacle Bible'. The use of 'treacle' to replace 'balm' subtly aligns evil with the snake, implying
that the balm that soothes the sin-sick soul dispels evil, much as
treacle's antidote dispels venom. But here, the 'bad' snake is
also the snake that heals (treacle is made from serpent flesh),
much as the bad Edenic snake manifested the good Gnostic
saviour and much as the patristic light world was fashioned
from the matristic dark serpentine body.

A concurrent medicine, associated with Venice treacle,
called 'mummy', emerged in the thirteenth century. This was a
strange trade in human remains: mummified bodies and dried
and pounded skull, brain, heart, hair, blood or urine. A brisk
business in this debris flourished, lasting, in some parts of the

world, until the nineteenth century. Many severe illnesses, such as epilepsy, paralysis or eye troubles, were treated with 'mummy'. When mixed with Venice treacle, it cured ulcers, skin problems and general withering. Snakebite was also treated at the time using human saliva.

Venice treacle entered alchemy. In the fifteenth century, arch alchemicist Paracelus revised and simplified Andromachus' theriaca into his *Laudanum Paracelis*, a highly popular remedy. The name reveals, though, that Venice treacle was turning toward the narcotic. In the sixteenth century, while van Helmont expounded his 'irritated spirits' theory, French apothecary Moise Charas busied himself in his dispensary, *The Golden Serpent*, making every possible variation of the real serpent-based theriaca as well as Orvietan (which was less complex). He took raw or cooked snakes and mashed, burned, distilled, drowned and boiled them into potions, pastes, poultices, electuaries and pills.[4]

During the plague years, a 'good Venice treacle' could be blended with fumitory, a herb which contained components usable as a tonic, skin cleanser and blood purifier, or with scabious, taken in Europe for expectoration and against leprosy (an interesting link to the Persian theriaca). Their detoxifying sweat made a prophylactic. Culpeper also suggested Venice treacle with the herb tormentil, a mix considered the superdrug against super maladies such as poisoning, plague and the pox:

Tormentil is most excellent to stay all fluxes of blood or humours, whether at nose, mouth or belly. The juice of the herb and root, or the decoction thereof, taken with some Venice treacle and the person laid to sweat, expels any venom or poison, or the plague, fever or other contagious disease, as the pox, measles, etc., for it is an ingredient in all antidotes or counterpoisons . . .

Daniel Defoe, in his account of 1665, the *Journal of the Plague Year*, tells how 'several times [I] took Venice treacle, and a sound sweat upon it, and thought myself as well fortified against the infection as any one could be fortified by the power of physic'.[5]

The serpent links continued in covert references. Englishman William Lilly, in his 1647 *Christian Astrology*, attributes Venice treacle to Mercury, the god who holds the dualistic caduceus, a link made no doubt through the snake. Mercury, too, rules scabious astrologically.

In the eighteenth century, Venice treacle took a sinister turn to the soporific. Samuel Johnson refers to it as the 'killing nurse' because it was used to 'quiet' babies to death in the workhouse. It was also nicknamed 'Lord have mercy upon me!' to under-score the false dismay these murders elicited. It was a regular part of any household's medicine chest, though liquid lau-danum, now Venice treacle's obvious cousin (and cheaper to buy than alcohol), often replaced it. Along with rue, garlic, ale and pewter filings, it was in Irish and English recipes against the bite of rabid dogs. It treated bilious colic. American newspapers advertised Venice treacle for sale along with borax, laudanum, castor oil and many other herbal and pharmaceutical remedies.

By the nineteenth century, Venice Treacle was essentially an opiate. Nevertheless, Sir Walter Scott, in his 1821 novel *Kenilworth*, recalled a Venice treacle of old when he returned it to its former glory as the 'sovereign remedy against poison', an opin-ion 'once universally received by the learned as well as the vulgar'.

Current Chinese medicine uses serpent to treat the same illnesses and problems Venice treacle and like remedies addressed: aches, back pain, arthritis, rheumatism, premature ejaculation, impotence, depression, insomnia, poor appetite, neurasthenia, sadness, coughing, shortness of breath, acne and

An ancient method of healing, still in use today in Turkey, is to wrap a snake around the head.

skin irritation. A snake's gall bladder, the base for a universal cure-all, is sometimes applied with sesame oil on infected skin. It is also used against fever, asthma and allergies.

Almost ailment for ailment, Amerindians have used rattlesnake in healing in much the same way as the Asians and Europeans used viper. Navahos sing a 'Beauty Chant' against snakebite, but other health problems intercepted by this chant are similar to those cured by Venice treacle: rheumatism, sore throat, and difficulties with kidney, bladder and stomach. Rattlesnake was effective as a treatment for headaches, either by tying the skin or the rattle around the head or even wrapping a live snake. People experimenting with alternate methods of healing have revived this practice. (The Romanians connect snakes and headaches in a story of a snake's own head pain cured by having its head crushed.) The meat was used for chest problems such as tuberculosis and emphysema. The skin was sometimes dried into a power and taken as a blood cleanser. The Sioux appreciate the rattlesnake as a cousin, taking its rattle warning as a gesture that allows for good neighbours. They won't kill them because an ancient story tells of four brothers, three of whom transformed into giant rattlesnakes. When the fourth enlisted their help before war, the snakes offered a medicine bundle that protected him and the tribe for generations. Mexican Indians used rattler fat as an analgesic and to reduce tumours and swelling. The oil was made into a salve for aches, including arthritis and rheumatism, and for skin ailments such as sciatica. Snake's gallbladder was mixed with chalk and used as an oral electuary for fever and smallpox.

An interesting aspect to this long palliative international lineage is that its base ingredient, the viper body, however distilled over the centuries, remained a magic healer, as it had in ancient and prehistoric times. The snake, as a real or imaginary substance, retains power to combat the most frightening of harms – poisons, cancers and plagues. In a sense, it cheats death. Just as the snake ghost sat unconsciously in the Greek mind, the snake as guardian, as resurrector, as rejuvenator, as healer and as catalyst – dominant attributes of the chthonic serpent divinity – lie within all these remedies. They promote the ambiguity of the good and bad creation snake where the villain and hero combine, or where, as in the caduceus, the poison and the antidote are one. This is echoed in seventeenth-century's English preacher Jeremy Taylor's dictum: 'We kill the viper, and make treacle of him.'

4 Edible Snake

Oddly, though oysters, snails, squid, octopus, eel, brains, testicles, tongue, tripe, kidneys, snout, trotters and many other potentially peculiar foods are devoured without a second's thought, half the world shudders at the idea of eating snake, allotting it the euphemism given to squeamish food: 'it tastes like chicken'. But does it? The rich meat of the Japanese sea krait, Senegalese python, Indian cobra, Italian viper, American rattlesnake or Brazilian boa, smoked, barbecued, fried or fermented, is cooked with gusto around the world. Its consistency has been likened to a tender calamari or conch if steamed correctly. The East gobbles it up but the West rarely abides its flesh. Yet, throughout history, European, Middle Eastern and American lore has reverenced the edible snake as enchanted, imbuing the eater with extraordinary talents.

In the epic German poem, the *Nibelungenlied*, written about 1200, the young warrior Siegfried, having killed the serpent-dragon, Fafner, bathes in and tastes its blood and eats its heart. In absorbing the blood and organ, he 'knows all mysteries', becomes telepathic and can speak with birds and animals. The heart offers virtually the same gifts as that of the Sioux Uncegila's, which bestowed clairvoyance and absolute governance, and whose superlative blood restored sight to the blind hero who killed her. The *Nibelung* story is only one of an abundant lore on the magic of eating ophidian flesh, especially the heart. Though seemingly only a token of the greater symbolic snake, the edible snake is actually equitable, able to yield the same wisdom, youth, immortality, health, sexual vigour, vision of truth, supernatural power, second sight, telepathy and access to other worlds. The origin of this belief is unknown but it certainly appears in early Egypt, when Ra is renewed from his battle with one serpent by travelling daily, as if consuming it, through the body of another called 'Life of the Gods'. But a different story may reveal why 'heart' and 'omniscience' became identified as one: in the Egyptian imagination, they were identical. Isis, wanting to be the 'mighty goddess' fashioned a snake out of her spit and dust and had it bite and poison the ageing Ra. She refused him help until given his arcane, unspeakable name within which lay all his omnipotence and, as such, was his very heart. When he consented to reveal it, his heart-name left him, entered her and she usurped him. The Sioux story of Uncegila also concentrates total world command in the serpent heart, suggesting that it is a widespread association. The edible snake may go further back in time but whatever its beginning, the inheritance is clear. The stories, however modified, re-enact the foremost roles of the mythic snake as resurrector, channeller and healer.

The notion of eating a snake and being eaten by one blend around ideas of renewed life. The resurrected person's emergence from an open serpentine jaw is a globally recurrent image. As a version of the self-consuming uroboros, folklore holds that snakes eat their young as a protection and regurgitate them when danger ends. Egyptians cited this fantasy 4,000 years ago and it appears in Spenser's sixteenth-century epic *The Faerie Queene.* A millennium before the *Nibelungenlied* was written, Pliny revealed similar protections to be had in the meat of the dragon, a creature he generically classified as 'a huge serpent'. He recommended bathing in its blood as a cure-all and extolled the eating of its sun-dried fat as a guard against ulcers. He also believed that if a dragon's baby was killed, the mother could restore it to life. The serpent-dragon, so dominant in ancient Greek mythology, was an accepted animal in Roman consciousness and Pliny incorporates these views into his voluminous *Natural History*, a medical reference (and an alchemical one) well into medieval times. In a sense, Eve comes to wisdom through an edible snake who by proxy offers not snake flesh but the substitute forbidden apple of knowledge. Knowing is still acquired by eating. The first-century AD neo-Pythagorean charismatic preacher Apollonius of Tyana, born in Anatolia, and considered by many contemporaries on a par with Jesus, ate the heart of a serpent to become a savant. Arabs were thought prophetic and able to decipher bird language, according to Philostratus, because they consumed snakes' hearts and livers. The Oxford scholar and occultist Michael Scott gained sagacity in the twelfth century from the 'juices' of a white snake. On cooking it, he burned his fingers and, sucking on them, suddenly tasted knowledge. The nineteenth-century Scots revised the story to fit that of a young boy who grew into Brochdarg, Prophet of the North. Given a white snake to boil by his master, and warned not to eat it, he nevertheless licked his hot fingertips and became clairvoyant. Even up to the twentieth century, dervishes (such as Psyllis who converted to Islam in the 1100s) half-swallowed live snakes as a way to suck out their influence. Sindhi patron saint of snakes, Gogol Vir, though human, was so suffused with serpent consciousness that when a snake mortally bit him, he told his son to cook and eat his own body. Before the boy could consume the boiled meat, thieves devoured it and instantly gained magical art and control over serpents.

The Britons believed that drinking serpent broth produced super-natural talents and the Chinese still consume snake soup as a supernal panacea. Conversely, the Hopi derive enlightenment from refusing snake flesh. Because they regard the snake as a divine messenger, there is an absolute ban on eating the animal.

Already intimately associated with the elixir of life, the edible snake also confers immortality. In another version of the allegorized snake from the 'Hole in the Stone' bestiary story that regenerated itself from sin as 'young and fresh', the eaten snake brings new life. Ra's rejuvenation through figuratively devouring the serpent's body was repeated thousands of years later in John Fletcher's 1625 English comedy, *The Elder Brother*. He declared that

> You can eat a snake
> And are grown young, gamesome and rampant.

This promises not only youth but, with it, ready sexuality. An early twentieth-century story, told in Greece, recounts a dying tubercular Swede who came upon a white liquid in a rock, which he drank. As soon as a huge snake loomed, the man real-ized it was snake's vomit but felt a surge of outlandish strength and found his illness healed.

All of these legends show ancient serpent traces: the snake which transforms is a carry-over of the snake whose presence resurrects; the snake who rejuvenates is the serpent initiating the neophyte into a new life; the devoured snake revealing another level of communication is like the underworld guide who slides between the divine and earthly with ease; snake blood that opens the senses and snake flesh that confers wisdom, makes one young or restores vigour are the immortal and omniscient serpent. Strange as they are, these ideas are still active. Asia consumes snake not only as a meal but as an aphrodisiac and immunity fix. These contemporary versions of an elixir of long life mirror the themes of Euro-American-African myths.

But the myths of these regions don't match their gastronomy. European, American and African cuisine do not typically use snake, though there are places, such as Cameroon, Albania and the American Southwest where serpent dishes are known. But in Asia, from Vietnam and China to New Guinea and India, snake is a beloved morsel, often as a combination of different species such as cobra, krait and boa, and cooked in every way conceivable. These dishes (and snake medicine) are so loved that recent government controls in countries like Vietnam and China stopped the lucrative snake export in 1999 because the species was being decimated and the rat population had nearly tripled. However, in 2003 the law was lifted. Many restaurants operate their own snake farms to avoid these kind of sanctions. Snake dishes aren't easily accessed outside Asia. A prohibition on public snake cuisine exists in some Western cities, probably because of a fear that snakes will escape. But, despite the difficulties, some places will supply the needy customer. For example, a tiny four-table restaurant, the only one out of a vast New York Chinatown district, makes snake available as a special soup for medicinal purposes, served only in the fall. Autumn is the season when snake is best eaten as the young are grown and hibernation is imminent. Frozen snake, always unnamed, is frowned on as inferior but is commonly sold.

The Chinese, with a cuisine steeped in 'ye wei' or 'wild flavour' including odd animals (to a Westerner) such as civet cat, bear, bat and monkey, are notorious for eating anything that flies, swims, walks, slides or crawls. Their snake cookery is traceable to the Han Dynasty and snake meat is adored. Boas are favourites. The Chinese eat their way through some 10,000

Snake *haute cuisine* in a specialist restaurant, 1986.

The snake market in China, 2003.

Skinning a snake before cooking, 1986.

tons of snake annually. Guangzhou (formerly Canton) province is especially renown for non-spicy snake specialties. Hong Kong is also replete with savoury options. The restaurant Yung Kee offers hot fried snake skin, snake and abalone, deep-fried snake meat balls, snake sausages, and a famous five-kinds-of-snake soup known as 'The Dragon, the Tiger and the Phoenix' which uses cobra, sea krait and rat snake mixed with civet cat or lamb and chicken. The 2,000-year-old recipe is robust with spices, sugars, fruits and ham stock, boasting sugar cane, ginger, dried longans, brown or red dates, thirty year old mandarin peel, shredded lemon leaves, chrysanthemum petals and flakes of a crouton-like pastry made from egg and flour.[1]

Japan eats and exports smoked sea snakes and relishes sake steeped in the poisonous habu. Taiwan is also known for serpent cuisine but Vietnamese cooking, extensively using the animal, is the most famous and delicious, as this author found. Often cooked with other meats, such as chicken or fish heads, ham, abalone or pork strips, snake is delicately accented with fragrant herbs, fruits, and vegetables and accompanied by dipping sauces, such as sesame, that boost the flavours. Whole villages subsist through the selling of a snake from food to drink – snake blood, snakeskin, snake liver, snake heart, snake flesh, snake ribs, snake bile and snake wine – to produce a meal as large as ten courses. Hanoi's Snake Village district, and the narrow streets of the nearby town of Le Mat, are famous for speciality restaurants where snakes, big and little, poisonous and non, kept on the premises in cages or cloth bags or even left free in trees, are killed at the table and, adhering to ancient recipes, are grilled, roasted, sautéed, boiled, stewed, browned, broiled, or fried into anything from crispy snacks to hash. Sour snake mash or snake with lemon or browned in fat are always in demand, as is snake skin, steamed or crisped, which is good for the complexion. The street markets also serve snake, skinning the animal alive (sometimes taking two men to hold it), draining its blood, chopping it in pieces, flashing it through a blazing wok, and pouring it into a bowl – in minutes.

Snake liquors are all claimed as *the* drink for longevity and *the* virility enhancer. Old people and men are the typical tipplers. Though virility is explicit in China's 'Five Penis Wine', made with penises of snake, dog, sheep, deer and bull, a more typical drink is mixed from freshly killed cobra blood dripped into rice wine and drunk immediately. Fat jugs or slender bottles of strong greenish wine, called viperine, where steeped serpents visibly coil, line the markets, bars and restaurants. To make it, a live snake (or three different kinds) is submerged in concentrated alcohol with herbs. After three days, once the poison has been drawn, the snake is removed, its head cut off, body drained of blood, and insides gutted. It is then returned to 40 proof liquor and aged for at least 100 days (sometimes in buried bottles). The poisonous versions are the most coveted but all are considered good for libido, backache, rheumatism and ageing. Occasional but less effective is liquor made from snake baked to a yellow colour, dried and soaked in alcohol. But the most frightening drink to a foreigner is *rou tiet ran*, which consists of a raw heart. A customer can take a shot of vodka (or wine) in which a still beating, live cobra heart has been dropped. In Indonesia, this drink is known as 'Viagra in a glass'. If that's too much to bear, one can chug vodka suffused with pinkish cobra blood or green cobra bile or snake foetus instead. There is even a black Vietnamese wine made from fermented birds (feathers included) that eat snakes. Westerns have described these liquors as delicious and potent, sometimes like a Bloody Mary, sometimes like rare roast beef, and always a perfect companion to a serpent dish.

Snake wine, 2004.

REAL SPECIALITY OF VIE...
SNAKE WINE (...

USAGE ... RHEUMATISM...

The Edenic snake is still aphrodisiacal: catwalk models as Eve and Adam carrying Viagra, New York, 2003.

Snake liquor is sometimes drunk in the West and snake meat is eaten in some American states; rattlesnake especially is a Southern and Southwestern delicacy. It is typically barbecued, deep fried, made into chilli or curry, stew, soup or sausage but can be inventively served (as the recipe for empañadas in the Recipe section shows) and a desire to tenderize its chewy consistency is yielding sophisticated recipes. Some think snake is best when slow cooked. But regional dish or not, it's always unusual. A Californian swore that as a teenager in the 1970s he ate at a drive-in restaurant called Snake-a-Rama in Los Angeles which featured snake cuisine as a novelty. Snakes such as cobra and rattlesnake can be ordered from exotic meat purveyors; most of these cuts go to Asian communities, the rest to the adventurous. Snakes are raised in Arizona and Texas specifically for these demands. Snake meat is an expensive item, up to £20 ($40) per lb (0.5 kg). (Some international snake recipes and cocktails are listed on pp. 202–6.)

Snakes appear in food, as everywhere else, as a magical name, from 'Viper' gum to ex-Grateful Dead guitarist Bob Weir's 'Snake Oil Stir Fry and Otherworld Wok Sauce', which he named in honour of the old snake-oil salesman products. In Italy, the *pizelle*, one of the country's oldest known cookies, originated at their Festival of the Snakes, to celebrate the success of driving serpents from the town. Morocco cooks a sweet almond pastry known as the snake or *m'hanncha* that mimics a serpentine form. In India, at the end of August, the Punjabi Mirasan make a snake out of dough and take it from house to house. Offerings of food are given and when every house has participated, the dough snake is buried. In mid-September, women bring curd offerings to the grave and their children are given the leftovers.

5   Pet Snake

Pet snakes are now more stylish than ever but they have long been viewed as part of domestic life. As far back as Neolithic times, the snake protected hearth, home, and health. The ancient Greeks kept a sacred snake guardian in Athene's Parthenon, believing it to be the reincarnation of Gaia's snake son Erichthonius and equal to the Delphic Python. In many countries the snake was a household divinity and in Rome, Greece and Crete often kept as a pet to guard the home and rid it of mice. These associations still continue. In West Africa, the snake, incarnating an ancestor, protects the house and brings fortune. Snakes in India remain house deities and are left bowls of milk to drink. Fanatical murderer Charles Manson forbade his followers, at their desert Spahn ranch, to kill any snakes, feeling it was bad karma. Greek peasants still lure a wild snake into their house with milk because it brings good fortune. Until recently, Lithuania commemorated a 'Day of the Snakes' in early February. Holiday food was cooked to draw snakes into households in hopes that they would eat. If they did, the year would be blessed. Similarly, old Ireland held something like a modern Groundhog Day. When the hibernating snake, an aspect of Bride (or Brihgit), goddess of fire and culture, emerged in February on 'Bride's Day', serpent and Bride would inaugurate the spring.

A pet python slithers from a British toilet, 1998.

Fiction particularly enjoys three kinds of snake pets: the wanderer, the murderer and the guardian. Urban legends tell of a pet snake who emerges from a neighbor's toilet or of a snake sent in the mail or left in a mailbox for vengeance. In a sense, the murderous and guardian snake dovetail into one because the killing can save the owner or owner's friends. These two roles are implicit in animals such as the Delphic Python or the Nordic Fafner who defend a being or substance through intimidation, as well as in the multitude of snakes sent by avenging gods. The latter-day murderous pet usually wreaks havoc on hapless victims. The riveting 1913 French film serial *Fântomas* featured the Phantom, a master criminal who revelled in vicious crimes. For unusually difficult jobs (and he was *very* adroit) his pet boa, called the Silent Executioner, was sent to kill. A favourite ophidian murderer is the tiny venomous snake, slipped into a person's pocket or bed. The first wrong gesture leads to death. This device provided the denouement for the otherwise light-hearted 1955 film *We're No Angels*, starring

A horned viper, the snake most likely to have been Cleopatra's asp, from a 1550s collection of *Observations du Plusieurs Singularitez et Choses Memorables*.

Humphrey Bogart and Aldo Ray as convicts escaped from Devil's Island. Ray carried his beloved little snake, Adolph, in case it was needed and, at the film's end, it poisoned their persecutor. The Italian *Black Cobra* (1976) starring Jack Palance and *Emmanuelle* lead Laura Gemser delivered a particularly gruesome vengeance when Gemser forced a black cobra up a man's rectum (with the fantastical statement that it would 'eat' its way out of his body) in revenge for her friend's death. In Roman times, when suicide was believed to be noble, a snake assisted. Cleopatra, the last Egyptian monarch of a culture colonized for 300 years by Greece, used this method as her final out when she placed a viper on her skin.

In the 1980s, pet snakes became a multi-million dollar industry. They can be costly. A pair of Angolan python babies can run over £2,500 ($5,000) but an enthusiast can expect to pay anywhere from £30 ($60) to £250 ($500) for a range of other species like ball pythons, Japanese rat snakes or milk snakes. Who is a snake pet enthusiast? Every kind of person it seems – rich and poor, female and male, young and old. The famous love them: Rudolph Valentino and his wife, designer Natacha Rambova, kept a gopher snake. The disaffected love them: illicit snakes are often found in lonely apartments. Snakes are no

A Chinese woman who spent 153 days living in a snake house in Happy Valley Park, China, 2002.

longer just a secret hobby or a child's phase but have become a worldwide passion. The pleasure is in the animal's beauty or, for some, the symbolic cachet of ownership.

Astoundingly, many venomous snakes are kept as pets including the Gaboon viper, the rattlesnake, copperhead (most common in the US), and the cobra. Though a permit is sometimes obtainable, it is usually illegal to keep a poisonous snake, but this rule is impossible to enforce. In 1999, in a Delaware apartment, a decomposed man was found surrounded by lethal serpents. Some men keep poisonous snakes as a sign of manhood. An American career soldier in the 1920s was known to have a box of rattlesnakes under his marriage bed to, as he put it, 'toughen him up'. Of course, religious groups such as the Signs Following also hold snakes on their property but as livestock. Some owners have been known to tame their venomous

snakes and certainly that is a quality of all snake handling. But even non-venomous snakes pose problems. An incident in 1997, when a pet boa ate a neighbour's chihuahua, drove the New York City Council to rule that all snake owners must have a permit but, again, who can enforce it? In another New York incident, in 1996, a Burmese python crushed a teenager because he had underfed it. A child was eaten for similar reasons by a pet python in Burma in 1972.

A man inside a 35-foot-long giant anaconda, captured and killed after eating him.

Pythons and boas are favourites as pets, as are harmless common snakes such as the king, gopher and garter because of their beautiful colouring and patterns. Some owners feel that snakes require little care since they are sluggish (though some are active) and have no emotional responses. But care can be expensive and time-consuming. There should be dappled light and a specially lit hot-spot where snakes can bask. Because they don't pant or sweat, snakes can get too hot or dry so the temperature must be constant (at 70–80°F), often with 24-hour humidifier and nightly sprays of water by hand. Matting or wood chips should coat the floor and plants are vital for oxygen and green hideaways. Structures as high as 2 metres (6 ft) can be necessary so a snake can climb. Without this exercise muscles atrophy. A pool is vital. All snakes can swim and most like to lie in water. The cage needs constant cleaning.[1] Snake food is typically pre-killed (defrosted mice, rats, rabbits) because as well as causing terror to the prey, a fight between the two could cost the snake an eye. But some owners relish the battle scene. Cases such as the one in Delaware occur if a snake expects food when the cage opens and thus bites.

Snakes are susceptible to diseases carried by mites, worms or parasites. In the wild, a snake can fend these off but it can succumb in captivity. Zoos typically construct their herpetoriums around an interior room into which no unofficial person is permitted for fear of contagion. The snake's fragility in the face of disease causes people to buy farm-bred animals and these farms are common around the world. But it is not difficult to breed your own snakes at home. Eggs placed in a box in a closet, with a regulated temperature, will hatch and, as highlighted in Chapter 1, the degree of heat will determine the sex of the animals.

Stress of captivity can be overwhelming, especially in zoo life, and most zoos have very old reptile houses. As new attractions they were first built around the late 1900s but typically today's serpentoriums date back to the 1930s and many have not been renovated. The buildings can be excessively hot and dry, poorly ventilated and permeable to bacteria or parasites.

Care in the reptile house is usually of little concern to the public, but neglect can become obvious. A serpentorium in New York's Long Island, after much activist lobbying, was closed in 2003 for inhumane conditions.

There are numerous herpetological societies around the world (some are listed under web sites in the bibliography), that protect serpents and aim to conserve and educate. Their expertise can range from the capture of wild snakes which have entered homes (in snake-ridden areas), and the rescue of a discarded pet, to new findings in science and changes in legislation. Numerous international museums and institutes are dedicated to snakes and top universities are avidly researching serpent habits and venoms.

A spacious new Reptile House in London Zoo, from the *Illustrated London News*, December 1851.

6 Vogue Snake

The snake has always been, and remains, a vogue item, be it as diversion, pet, clothes, art, cuisine or militia. Much of the abundant heritage of serpent symbolism has deteriorated into cartoon meanings but our continuing attraction to serpents is an interesting element of magical cultural thinking. The snake in vogue is not the religious snake but the former is a tangent of the latter. Yet the vogue snake, less about divinity and more about prestige, is steeped in ancient holdovers found in such models as the serpentine line, the avenging pet snake, snake *femme fatale*, snake hero and snake clothing.

Because of these, or despite them, the snake now is something that entertains. It is a companion, a sensual signature, a mesmerizing spectacle. But the question is, at what level? Sex and death are still today's snake themes but, in the last few centuries, certain snakes of antiquity have emerged as especially potent modern icons. Many are rooted in Romantic imagery, and its high distortion of the original archaic serpent meaning, yet the influence on culture has been huge. They have guided the Western mind toward blunt sex–death/female–male snake correspondences. Some prevalent tropes are found in Medusa's snake-hair and paralyzing look; Laocoon, the Trojan who, along with his sons, was strangled by serpents; Cleopatra and her suicide by asp; and the defeated villain serpent. But there is another side: that of a continuing ophidian integrity found in the serpentine line, a virtually unchanged symbol. It is the best place to begin looking at snake vogues.

This line, embodying action, process, life energy and continuity, is one of the most perfect expressions of a symbol *being* its idea. In the 13,000-year-old Palaeolithic Taï plaque, the serpentine line embodied the philosophical science that it inscribed. Its shape mirrored at once the universal system and the cosmic snake. In the late Renaissance, European art extended that same idea through theories around a sinuous, continuing linearity and the serpentine line has been since singled out for special notice in painting, drawing, sculpture, architecture, writing and science. The vital aspects of the mythic serpent – as initiator, creator, guide and energizer – subliminally animate the S-line though history.

French anthropologist Remo Guidieri has argued that three basic forms underlie architecture: one, the grid, made of cross hatched lines, which represents extension; two, the circle, which represents enclosure; and three, the serpentine line, which expresses free movement between both. The latter is visible in the West's twentieth-century forms, from Frank Lloyd Wright's winding Guggenheim Museum in New York to Frank Gehry's rolling and bulging Guggenheim in Bilbao. Another architect, Antoni Gaudí, used serpentine lines more impressively. Though his exteriors roil with decorative Art Nouveau curves, internally, and with some complication, Gaudi used free flowing S-forms to redistribute weight structurally, a difficult task. He returned the serpentine line to its metaphysical nature as a load-bearing force, almost as a mimic of the super snake underlying the cosmos.

These aesthetics have gestations in the sixteenth-century Italian Mannerist movement's expressive structures in architec-

The snake-matted head of Medusa in Benvenuto Cellini's 16th-century bronze of *Perseus*, a statue that uses the serpentine line to subtly guide all of its sculptural form.

ture, painting and sculpture. The Mannerists inaugurated the concept of the *figura serpentinata*, vibrant and disturbing shapes so groundbreaking that they launched the cult of 'art for art's sake' because, in the hands of artists like Cellini, Giambologna and Michelangelo, the importance of form suddenly trumped the importance of content. Cellini's young, naked *Perseus* angularly leaning his weight on one leg and holding up Medusa's severed, dripping head is a prime *figura serpentinata* example.

Though Donatello had tapped into the idea in the fifteenth century, it was the unearthing in Rome of a sculpture of Laocoon and his sons struggling with coiling serpents that changed everything. Its portrayal of action through curling shapes influenced Michelangelo enormously and he began to work with a new wild line, based on the serpent's arabesque. His experimentations with sculpture, as Giorgio Vasari described, 'broke the fetters' of previous tradition. Classic plasticity was refashioned into an exuberant, twisted but refined form, freezing an act in motion to make the sculpture as close to movement as possible. The

The overt serpentine line in the 1st century AD Greek sculpture of Trojan priest Laocoon and his sons attacked by snakes sent as a divine punishment.

Mannerist felt that their art, guided by the S-line, became part of living time. To do this, they wrought the continuous serpentine shape around three dimensions, a line so fiery it compelled the viewer to examine front, side and back of the statue. Ideally, passive observation was no more. The exciting serpentine line roused the viewer and encouraged a full awareness of what was being seen. The viewer was moved to move (around the piece) and as s/he moved, time was lived. The art then lived too. This echoes the primary cosmic serpent: the S-line joins living (awareness) with eternity (art); it releases the passive into the active (gaze becomes engaged); it engenders, like Sakti, a raised consciousness (the excited viewer).

The Mannerist agenda around the serpentine line rolled, covertly, through the curlicues of the Baroque and Rococo. In the eighteenth century, the line became the focus of theory again when British painter William Hogarth extolled it in his 1753 *Analysis of Beauty*, which examined the S-line as the quintessence of aesthetics. A century later, Van Gogh's fundamental wavy stroke wormed a new path toward modern art and even, as painter André Lhote regarded it, opened (as the S-line had done for centuries) the 'unconscious'.[1] Matisse and others worked that line into theories of colour, where colour, not linearity, acted the line's dynamism.

In much the same way, the serpentine line underlay the most ambitious writing manifestos. The nineteenth-century French Symbolist poet Stéphane Mallarmé advocated it almost mystically. He *heard* its look. To him the serpentine line was the simulacrum of music's effect on the perception and he wanted to evoke that indescribable rhythmical energy in his words' sound, alliteration and assonance. The assonant S-line's arabesque was 'complete', a bridge of danger and elegance connecting a precarious synapse between fear of the unknown and a primal recognition of it, which Mallarmé described as 'dizzying leaps in a terror that recognizes'.[2] His writing, full of complex, innovative rhythms worked into tiny vowel and consonant sounds, was structured on the same principle. Words and their sounds, not ideas, built the construct, much as motion, not subject, built Mannerism, and the *S*-line, not its decoration, formed Gaudí's buildings.

In all these painting and writing theories, there is a sense that, through the *S*-line, core art is reached. Though these ideas were not referenced by mythic antiquity, they nevertheless derive from the serpent's zenith: key to the unknown, initiator of creativity (life), and leader from one era (time zone) to another.

With so much capacity, advertising has inevitably stolen the serpentine allure. Snakes and their shapes, never out of fashion, share a special division. The line is seductive in and of itself, soothing yet invigorating, but most images exploit the public's fear of and fascination with snakes, using themes that touch on vague ideas of what serpent symbolism is: dangerous, exotic, sexual, forbidden, etc. These translate into contra-points between what the viewer is seeing and what the viewer is being asked to buy. The advertising snake bewitches while, as Dickinson said, it makes a 'tighter breathing' and 'zero at the bone'. The implication is that the product will do the same, inspiring breathless astonishment, envy and desire from those who have not bought what the buyer now owns.

Even television car ads appropriate this. A car is often sold as a luxury escape rather than as an automobile and can be filmed from the air sensuously zooming around winding roads. Its freedom and excitement blends into its control on difficult drives and the *S*-line lends an emotional frisson to the armchair viewer. The 1934 French ad for Heyraud shoes takes the serpent form into a similar promise, one of urbanity in the guise of play-

The resurrecting ophidian mouth reappears in this 1934 French advertisement for Heyraud shoes.

"tentation"

HEYRAUD

"ses chaussures en reptiles"

fulness. The snake, posed in a threatening, ready-to-spring coil, with blood red blobs on its back, is both animal and animation of the shoes made from its skin. The head has become a shoebox and the two shoes emerging from its open mouth are like a forked tongue. By configuring it as an eager, tail-wagging puppy holding out slippers the snake's ferocity has been dumbed down. As the giddy dog, the shoes comfort and as the alert snake, they transform. The resurrecting, open-jawed serpent appears, proffering 'new life' to the consumer and giving the lucky buyer serpentine snap.

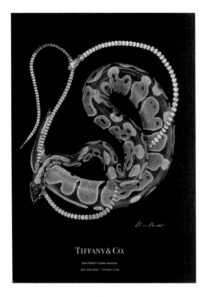

Tiffany jewellery
displayed as on
par with the
perfect, timeless,
beguiling snake.

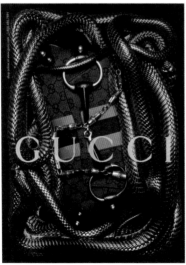

Snake as Gucci
intrigue.

But the live snake, wrapped over objects or the human body, is the punchiest of all. Jewellery is perhaps the most common product that the snake is asked to sell. In the 2003 Tiffany and Co. advertisement, the snake's fine reticulation and gorgeous pattern mirror the jewellery's workmanship, seen as a natural perfection transcending artificiality. The savvy buyer, by knowing what is truly worthwhile, has the same reflected qualities. Equally, the ad evokes fabled riches, defended by snakes, only accessible to the chosen and daring. Fashion designer Tom Ford's last show for Gucci in 2004 was heavily serpent themed. His magazine ads play on the deadly, cunning snake by showing Ford's accessories, such as belts and shoulder-strap purses, in a dark, tangled mass where a snake loops around the frame. It is well known that Ford, having served Gucci for years, was forced out of his position and the ad's black claustrophobic scene, reminiscent of intrigue, may reflect Ford's sense of a Machiavellian plot. The buyer is appealed to, however, as in the Tiffany advertisement, as a modern hipster made hipper by primitive sleekness. Here the emphasis is on a guarded hoard seen through a wary viewfinder.

A fear of snakes, and how that translates into prejudice, underlies all serpent iconography and is part of the modern appropriation of ancient images. Ophidiophobia is primal. A Dahomeyan proverb sums up its range – 'A snake bit me, now I am afraid of a worm.' Recent cognitive studies have shown conclusively that terror of snakes is genetic. An inner-city child, never having seen a real snake, will register greater fear in its brain activity when shown a picture of a serpent than when shown one of a gun. Herpetologist Harry Greene verifies this in his account of his Malamute who, despite hurling herself at any animal to protect him, will shrink from a snake. People have been known to die of fright when bitten by a harmless serpent and one of the most common anxiety dream animals is the snake but interpretations of why this is vary. Folklore from every kind of culture is steeped in crazy stories of snakes that roll into hoops and chase people for miles, snakes that whistle, snakes that swallow their young, snakes that milk cows at night, snakes (called *chirrioneros*) that follow menstruating women, snakes that enter the mouth and slide down the gullet, snakes that penetrate vaginas and lay eggs in the womb, snakes that rape field workers or snakes that kill women in childbirth. Obviously, most of these are projections of nervous dread. Slander too has tapped this fear. Shakespeare said that slander's 'edge is sharper than the sword, whose tongue / Outvenoms all the worms of the Nile' (*Cymbeline*, III, iv). The contemporary term 'snakehead' names Chinese traffickers who smuggle people, for exploitative costs, across borders and oceans. The phrases 'he's a snake' or 'a snake in the grass' express duplicity. To 'cherish a snake in your bosom' signals ingratitude, as does the 'serpent's egg', a catchphrase of treachery:

> Therefore, think him as a serpent's egg
> Which, hatched, would (as his kind) grow dangerous.[3]

This stems from a Greek anecdote of a man bitten by a snake, which he had revived from freezing by warming it on his chest. Tales of the thankless snake who assaults a rescuer or a greedy one outwitted by a brave person are found from the Balkan states to African-American folklore to Amerindian stories. To 'snake' in surfing is a term of disrespect, meaning to surf too close to, and cut off, someone already riding a wave. 'Snake oil' signifies any con that makes outrageous claims and to 'pour snake oil' on something means any general deceit. It arose from snake-oil salesmen who sold fake snake-based medicines

to a gullible public in the nineteenth and early twentieth century. Now the term is a catch-all for every kind of legal fraud from pharmaceutical fakery to school legislation to religious scams to weak laws to major political negotiations. It's been appropriated by the computer world, specifically in respect to false cryptography, which decodes softwear already safeguarded against hacking. The fakery suggests that, in some underground fashion, the real snake (not the snake-oil version) still connotes true guardianship. Bad fortune befalls ears that have been 'serpent licked' because then the lickee will become prophetic, but at a price. Trojan Cassandra, while sleeping in Apollo's temple, had her ears licked by snakes after which she could foretell the future but only the terrible events. Teiresias too was said to gain his gift from snake-licked ears. Snake-eyes describes the worst roll of the dice, a double one, and is emblematic of all bad luck.

Steven Spielberg's *Raiders of the Lost Ark* (1981) played on the primality of ophidiophobia by making his intrepid hero snake phobic. Spielberg knew this would be an acceptable failing and

148

The snake as a
latter-day Devil
who fascinates
Mowgli in the
1965 Disney film
The Jungle Book.

Ophidiophobia is
one of the most
primal fears: a
courage test in a
closed globe with
snakes as part of a
reality-TV show.

The fearsome
snake pit in
Steven Spielberg's
1981 film *Raiders
of the Lost Ark.*

A crazed, stop-frame Medusa from Desmond Davis's 1981 film *Clash of the Titans*.

that the audience would identify with Jones when he said, looking at a hole filled with serpents where he thinks he's about to die, 'Why did it have to be snakes?' Madness is directly correlated with the 'snake pit', slang for the insane asylum. Anatole Litvak's 1948 film, *The Snake Pit*, underscores the horror of mental illness through a long crane shot, drawn slowly up from the main floor where agitated patients wander, to eventually dissolve into an image of hundreds of writhing snakes.

The snake-haired Medusa is so engrained in modern consciousness that it, and its category of 'Gorgon', appears as a synonym for 'fear' in a 1980 *Roget's Thesaurus*, along with 'bug-a-boo, ogre, scarecrow' and 'hobgoblin'. The others are easily traceable to fairy stories but Medusa is an odd choice. It may well be siphoned through Freud's association of the severed Medusa head with the male castration complex and male fears of female persecution and the vulva. Freud believed that women were what he called 'female eunuchs', that is, castrated men. Their genitals were not self-sufficient but instead the bloody detritus of a missing phallus. Out of the consciousness of a Romantic sensibility, and vastly far from the intentions of the actual Greek myth, his short 1922 essay, 'Medusa's Head', determines that the decapitated Medusa head represents the vulva. The vulva's opening (Medusa's mouth), its menstrual blood (bleeding from sliced head), and its curly hairs (snake-locks) stand for the severed penis of the 'castrated' woman. The vulva is presented as both inadequate living organism and paralyzing dead killer and Freud reflects male fear of castration in this allegedly vulvic image. Freud's use of the Medusa head seemingly anchored his theory in historical truth, but study of these old stories shows that his claims don't bear out the original intent. Jung, conversely, saw the Medusa as something primally personal, the 'whole self', but he rendered it as the Medusa jellyfish, the round face surrounded by floating and curling strands. In the 1980s, designer Gianni Versace was closer to the original meaning when he made Medusa his symbol, stating that his fashions would shock as she had once done. He took the head for what it was – at once an attraction and disturbance.

These converse emotions about the snake are played out in art, be it whimsically or ponderously. It is an intriguing question as to why the serpent has, in the last few centuries, become so associated with negative sexuality, mostly female but also male. What is interesting about these gender strictures is that, under the misogyny or the prowess, the exceptional strengths of the primordial feminized supernal snake is detectable and, in fact, still seems to be the driving force of the serpent attraction. The snake was long used as an aphrodisiac, in vegetable or reptile substances such as Dragon's Blood, a red resin extracted from palms (placed under the bed to cure impotent men), or in cobra-blood-tinged vodka or in Asian virility medicines. Women once slept in the Asclepius temple to promote fertility, and today in India touching nagakals – stone stele with coiled serpent motifs – should foster pregnancy. But the magic snake has passed from this climate of fecundity into a peculiar creature of sexual prejudice. Joseph Campbell argued that the snake evoked genitalia because of its phallic body and yonic mouth, and many lay people conclude that the source of ophidiophobia is a fear of the penis. Yet if shape is the culprit than why is the snake-shaped earthworm rarely given a phallic status? This selectivity suggests that these ideas are virility wishes rather than fears. In *The Cult of the Serpent*, Balaji Mundkur states that very little evidence shows sex (in gender terms) in any significant snake symbolism. Though snakes are inherent to fertility themes, Kundalini themes, and sexual tangents such as childbirth and even rape, other animals are used to point to sexuality *per se* such as the mink, fox, rabbit or monkey. After all, to the naked eye, a snake is sexless. Phallic and yonic imagery of snakes is uncommon even though supposition encourages the opposite. Jean Chevalier, in his *Dictionary of Symbols* (1969), toes the sexist line in his serpent entry. He assumes that ancient belief systems tally with modern ones and genders, without question, the snake's mythic body: 'the serpent discards its male appearance to become female, coiling up, entwining around, squeezing, throttling, swallowing, digesting, and sleeping'.

It's plausible to genderize the straight or coiled snake but Chevalier also presupposes an essential male (it becomes female) whose murderous aspect (she throttles, squeezes, swallows) or passive one (digesting, sleeping) is enacted by the female. However, Chevalier's prejudice becomes acute in his summary of her role: 'The she-serpent is the invisible serpent principle, which dwells in the lower levels of consciousness and the deeper strata of the Earth. It is secret and equivocal, its decisions are unpredictable and as swift as its transformations.'[4] Equivocal and unpredictable are rare attributes of the cosmic snake, if indeed they are ever found. However this is typical of calumny against women. The symbolic snake, as is overwhelmingly evident, is one of ascendance as well as descendance. It is the universal activator, the Kundalini force that rises to the highest consciousness, the daemonic resurrector and the avenue to the divine.

So derogatory in slander, the snake is coolness itself around virility. Cobra, viper, rattlesnake and anaconda are *de rigueur* in manly names, a tactic, as a way to absorb the desired animal, that is no less than sympathetic magic. Typically, the snake name occurs in death contexts, such as war, yet ironically it signifies prowess, a life strength. The US army invaded Afghanistan in search of Osama bin Laden in 2002, under the rubric of 'Operation Anaconda', a reference to this snake's well-known stealth. Helicopters called Cobras and teams called Vipers were deployed. In the First and Second World Wars the rattlesnake was an insignia for fighting units, as it had been during the American Revolution. The Symbionese Liberation Front, the extremist 1970s group in the USA who kidnapped heiress Patty Hearst, took a seven-headed serpent as their emblem. The snake is also the stand-in for any enemy, whichever way that might be construed. Many political cartoons use the snake to tar others be it as imperialist, radical, fascist, communist, rebel or many more. Snakes can name fairly innocuous items such as a Viper snowshoe, Viper snowmobile, and the like, be it bike frame, car paint, hot wax, rollbar, custom-made throwing knife, tanning bed, turbo nozzle, climbing tool, do-it-yourself hovercraft kit or tattoo machine. But it also quantifies

The snake as convenient villain: the American Republican party stomps out the snake of Radicalism in Grant Hamilton's 1919 cartoon.

The snake as convenient villain: 1970s American student protesters attack the snake of Imperialism with the gun of art. Poster Brigade, 1979.

hostile merchandise such as the Remington Viper Rifle or the
Viper police in-car video unit, security alarm or radar detector.
There is a Viper hunting blind, which hangs in branches. The
ads display it as battle ready, showing an armed man, in
fatigues, waiting, as the copy line indicates, in his 'favorite
ambush position'. There are Viper chewing gums, novelty
candies, muscle booster powders, health bars and even vacuum
cleaners (for the domestic macho-man). There are Viper go-
carts and, for sports car enthusiasts, vehicles such as the 2004
Dodge Viper and Ford Mustang Cobra.

The tattoo is an extension of the magical name taken to a
more committed level. Erich Neuman suggests that '*all* body
openings – eyes, ears, nose, mouth (navel), rectum, genital
zones – as well as the skin, have, as place of exchange between
the inside and the outside, a numinous accent for early man'.[5]

A surgically forked tongue taps into archaic snake power, 2003.

The tattoo plays an interesting development in that exchange and that numinosity. The flattened, inky tattoo snake (a steady but not inordinately popular mark) still retains its channelling authority, drawing one world into another. One of its most striking images was the nineteenth-century Catawba Indians' blacksnake as war tattoo on the back. Snake tattoos appear often in a basic threatening pose, sometimes as a compound animal of feline and serpent. But scarification, another urban vogue, takes the snake into new realms. A forked tongue has become part of the snake masquerade.

By the late nineteenth century, particularly through the influence of Europe's Symbolist painters, the snake became an icon for the *femme fatale*, a creature evolved out of, but departed from, the Romantic imagination. English Romantic writers Shelley, Keats, Coleridge, Wordsworth, Blake and Byron used serpent imagery in the style of their era with an emphasis on sex and evil. However, the snake image, beautiful and frightening in its virtuosity, contained contradictory feelings peculiar to their Romantic ideals. For example, Coleridge favourably compared Shakespeare's work to the 'movement of a serpent'. In 'The Rime of the Ancient Mariner', the 'loathsome' water snakes surrounding a trapped ship suddenly become 'blessed'. Byron called Shelley 'the snake'; Shelley called himself a snake in his poem 'To Edward Williams', and made a snake the 'spirit of good' in 'The Revolt of Islam', where the snake stood for an unrecognized saviour. The snake was frequently a symbol for rejuvenation or an expression of idealism, materialism or original sin.

The Romantics almost sado-masochistically perceived the world as alive with a sublime beauty so terrifying that it could kill. They felt that the poetic imagination could penetrate plain life and access the ethereal with words and that words could teeter, perilously, between the supernatural and the natural. This edge was much explored by them in snake associations. The Medusa head, emblematic of the cross between death and life, energy and stasis, dread and reverence, and even revolution and stability, all bound within a deathless and death-filled female vitality, was a Romantic convention. Her head was analogued by writers as diverse as Percy Shelley, Walter Pater, Algernon Swinburne, William Morris, Gabriel D'Annunzio and Goethe, and with different conclusions.

The snake theme ran so deep, that one of Romanticism's germinal treatises, *Laocoön, or, The Limits of Painting and Poetry*, written in 1766 by German dramatist G. E. Lessing, maintained the serpentine as the springboard to action. Lessing titled his work after the grim tale of Laocoon and his two sons but based his ideas on the same Greek sculpture that had thrilled Michelangelo. Lessing wondered if pain was essential to art's purpose and, if it was, argued that the success of its portrayal was the obvious dividing line between the verbal and plastic. Accepting pain as alive, he found words the superior conveyance because, as something that only stops time, painting or sculpture can never truly express that which lives. Though so vibrantly attempted in the *Laocoon* sculpture, the statue fell short of truth because it lacked intrinsic action. Words however are free agents, able to ride between agony (Laocoon's actual feeling) and beauty (art and life's transition). As 'articulate sounds in time', words create process, one word sequentially leading into, and replacing, the next. They are *part of* time, not its snapshot. Thus they are well suited to effect a living moment because they never cease to be at work. Though the *Laocoon* statue was chosen for its action and condemned for its inaction, its choice aligns the serpent (and *S*-line), as always, with life's *dasein*. For Lessing, the sculpture's serpentine curves fail to evoke true living feeling. But his two main points – the temporal as alive and its animation in the eternal (art) – are the snake's prime attributes as a time animal and Lessing's placement of movement and time in the aesthetic argument, through the stimulation of the serpent, so like the Mannerist agenda, returns to old connections. How it is that these artistic ideas incarnate archaic beliefs is impossible to trace but that they do is clear. Arguably, the *S*-line, already loaded with connotations reaching as far back as the Palaeolithic, is the provocateur, urging the mind to think of action, and all that it means, in abstract terms.

This surge translated easily into Shelley's poem 'On the Medusa of Leonardo da Vinci in the Florentine Gallery' (1819), where he described the relationship with beauty in serpentine terms and as the 'tempestuous loveliness of terror', visually revealed in the snake-haired Medusa. Though Shelley

Cleopatra's snake was once a purifier of sin.

is making a statement based on an opinion of an adulterated monster and not on a semi-divine force, there is something tinged with ancient ophidian awe in this brief definition. The snake's host of mythic powers rests in the words 'tempestuous', 'loveliness' and 'terror' because they link to so many emotions which snake worship must have engendered in the believer. This conflictive and eroticized 'tempestuous loveliness of terror' led directly to the nineteenth-century *femme fatale* and her twentieth-century counterpart, a woman whose consuming seduction of men was rife with serpent allusion but one which had lost all vitality.

As a part of the Fall and the contrivance of sin as sexual, the snake was tied to the caricature of the irresponsible woman, a theme toyed with in history by the repeated portraiture of a despairing Cleopatra holding her murderous asp. By the eighteenth century, Cleopatra was another classic *femme fatale*, a libertine with the world at her fingertips, whose destructive hedonism finally reduced her to suicide. But this was in utter contrast to how she had been viewed in antiquity and for centuries after. Through the 1500s, Cleopatra symbolized courageous martyrdom. As Lucy Hughes-Hallett recounts in her biography, Cleopatra's suicide was thought to redeem her, refining her lewdness because the 'only good woman is a chaste woman and the only chaste woman is a dead one'.[6] Early Christians viewed her death by serpent as cleansing her of promiscuity. Chaucer regarded her as a woman of virtue because she died for courtly love, the high convention of the Middle Ages. Though Dante threw her in hell and Boccaccio damned her as greedy, to Spenser, though 'wanton', she was 'high-minded' and to Shakespeare, admirable. Her lethal asp acts as a redeemer whose death aspect delivers sinlessness and purification.

This escape hatch vanished by the mid-1800s and the combination of snakes, death, sexuality and the *femme fatale* became hard-core misogyny. Bram Dijkstra noted in *Idols of Perversity*, his work on the concept of 'feminine evil', that woman and snake became one in the nineteenth-century European/American male imagination and no terms were more overused in that era than 'serpentine', 'sinuous' and 'snake-like'. Women 'were there to supply the fantasies and then to take the blame for them'.[7] The Romantic beauty, which arose from charged suffering or awesome fear became, in the icy pornography of painters like Fernand Khnopff, Félicien Rops and Franz von Stuck, a cruel lure that was only destructive. Their depictions of triumphant, staring young female nudes entwined with snakes or with tentacle things emerging from a belly button or vulva represented an uneasy, male, libidinal sensibility. The *femme fatale*'s attraction for painters like these was only deadly, had no redemption, no transfigurative inspiration. She consumed vampiristically. The Medusa verve evident in Shelley's exaltation had disappeared into a pathological fear of and lust for heterosexual sex.

George MacDonald's novel *Lilith* (1895) drew from this accepted idea by capitalizing on the eponymous pre-Eve snake-bird goddess and, in so doing, weirdly binding the *femme fatale* with the serpent as cosmic evil and saviour. In his story, a 'worm-thing', slithering from a blazing fireplace, resurrected the dead Lilith by entering her heart. As the 'central fire of the universe', it 'radiat[ed] into her the knowledge of good and evil, the knowledge of what she is'. Lilith and the serpent were one because 'she is herself the fire in which she is burning'. Her curse was that this 'Light of Life'[8] no longer lit her consciousness because she was only the destroyer, now separated, in these cultural reconstructions, from her ophidian creatrix side.

The *fin-de-siècle* Art Nouveau *femme fatale*, closely following the Symbolist *femme*, was an otherworldly voluptuary. She was super-nature and her deadly allure (read chthonic stature) was signalled by her serpentine attributes (a live snake or snake headband, bracelet or armlet). Her ungodly hatred of men extended to the paternal divine. Swinburne, though as much in love with her enviable supremacist anarchy as against it, described her as 'beautiful always beyond desire and cruel beyond words; fairer than heaven and more terrible than hell; pale with pride and weary with wrong-doing; a silent anger

A snake bracelet, made for Sarah Bernhardt after a design by Alphonse Mucha.

against God and man burns, white and repressed, through her clear features'.

In the early 1900s, this same woman sashayed across the movie screen with her long dark hair still streaming over her ghostly skin, her 'clear' features still gleaming, her lovers still lowly and her insignias still serpentine. But cinema's *femme fatale* also reclaimed her Symbolist nature when studio publicity 'leaked' that she was also, literally, a vampire. Her snake attributes already confused her with one because the vampire blurred with the snake through its lethal bite. Though a European staple, it was found around the world. The Chilean Araucanian Indians believed in Pihuechenyi, a winged serpent who sucked the blood of anyone asleep overnight in the forest. This hideous

Male sexual dread in the 19th century expressed as seductive, repulsive, serpentine super woman in *Istar*, an 1888 chalk drawing by Fernand Khnopff.

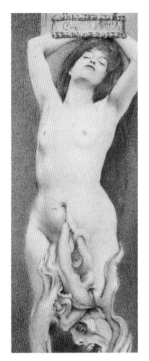

The snake-draped Symbolist *femme fatale* as coldly lethal in Franz von Stuck's oil painting *Sin* (1893).

Theda Bara, the first vamp, in telltale snake adornments, 1915.

A model replays the vamp look in 2002 through snake jewellery.

quality bizarrely heightened the screen siren's standing because it made her toxic sensuality dizzyingly perilous. By 1915, the 'vampire' femme was coined a 'vamp'. Her publicity touted this demonic personality as exotic to the point that some fans were mortally afraid of her. But this sado-masochistic attraction made her character all the rage and Theda Bara, the first vamp, had the right look. She paraded in Hollywood's notion of the ancient, that is animalized and semi-nude with blackened eyes, Egyptian slave girl clothing, snake jewellery posing with live snakes or with tangled hair pulled into snakish lines. Snakes signified her supra status but now as sexualized kitch.

Though she was preternaturally wild, the vamp was not an outdoors creature. Rather, in a weird twist on the archaic Snake Goddesses of hearth, health and time, she was an everlasting house woman, portrayed as a subversion of the true home. Her victim-lovers were received in her boudoir, parlour or hotel room, either one by one or in parties of worshipful swains. This was a nutshell universe where her control was total, her hospitality false and her domesticity a trap. In 1919, the Italian film, *La Piovra* (*The Octopus*), graphically underscored this peril by transforming silent screen diva Francesca Bertini into a rearing snake as she entertained her lover, now changed into a mouse. Throughout the 1920s, unscrupulous, snaky women vamped across the silver screen. Even in avant-garde French filmmaker Germaine Dulac's *La Belle Dame sans merci* (1921), the courtesan wore the tell-tale snake bracelet. In *Blood and Sand* (1922), Rudolph Valentino's first great success, Nita Naldi pitilessly seduced him, giving him a snake ring (once the property of Cleopatra) as a token of their love but representing his enslavement to her. In the plodding melodrama *Cobra* (1922), 'cobra' Naldi morally killed Valentino. Never stated, the serpent femme was coded in his hallucination of a snake ornament becoming a semi-nude woman, which the audience instinctively recognized. In keeping with the times, the film turned lust into a grave, setting up sex (outside of marriage) as aggression, committed by women whose satisfaction came more from psychic castration than from pleasured libido. These women were rarely, if ever, punished for their crimes against humanity. They were beyond caring, unreachably disinterested. These liabilities not withstanding, to possess the suave, sexy, insouciant danger that the snake represented, Valentino made the cobra his personal symbol, embellishing his cigarette cases, jewellery and car. In 1922, even T. S. Eliot played on the *femme fatale* in *The Waste Land*, when he wrote of an occult woman who directed strange activity through her snake-like hair:

A woman drew her long black hair out tight
And fiddled whisper music on those strings
And bats with baby faces in the violet light
Whistled, and beat their wings
And crawled head downward down a blackened wall . . .

The empowering *S*-line, so visually explicit, undulates through these and other crude demonstrations, by means of the *femme fatale* persona, of sex as power, certainly a throwback to the Great/Snake Goddess bond of carnality and omniscience. This homage unconsciously underlies the snake as cultural slang for seductress.

The vamp disappeared in the Art Deco era, replaced by her opposite: a thin, flat-chested flapper with short hair and ambition that took her far from home. However, the daunting serpent had not vanished. It pervaded the house, even if the *femme fatale* had left the scene, as snake-shaped jewellery, furniture, table wear and clothing. In the nineteenth century, Queen

An American
19th-century silver
snake pitcher
builds its form on
the supple beauty
of the serpentine
line.

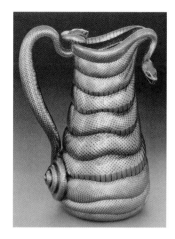

René Lalique's
glass snake vase,
1920s.

Edgar Brandt's
very popular
1920s 'Cobra'
gilt bronze and
alabaster floor
lamp.

Victoria's serpent engagement ring had popularized such shapes. Once its connotations leaned toward the *femme fatale*, it was refined into a deco staple for cases, pins, rings, bracelets and necklaces. Designer René Lalique was especially fond of this form creating figures such as a coiled snake with displayed fangs moulded into a misty glass vase or a gold inlaid brooch with rearing serpents. Edgar Brandt's floor lamp cast as a standing serpent with flickering tongue holding a globe became a principle of 1920s furniture.

The archaic Great Snake Goddess is visible in all of the above, even to draining virile blood from her consorts (such as was shed in the Meter cult). The 1910s and '20s diva and vamp, like the Snake Goddess, was earthbound yet cosmic, her body venereal and divine, her talismans serpents. Everything yielded to her greatness. The rapacious *femme fatale* was the chthonic inevitability of the Goddess triumvirate. Just as the uroboric round of the prehistoric Goddess held all time and all conception, the *femme fatale* held dominion over the 'indoors' as a microcosm of dominion over the universe. The Romantics retained some of her life energy but the Symbolists and subsequent portrayals deadened her. By the beginning of the twentieth century, she still reigned but only in the underworld.

However, despite these morbid depictions, the snake/woman iconograph did not lose its prehistoric balance of good and bad but spread across the arts in profoundly influential ways. Its fascination, arguably, continued to lie within the lure of the *S*-line, which, like the apotropic Medusa head and the intransigent, exciting *figura serpentinata,* repelled as it compelled; an arousing interplay often taken to extremes. Thus rising alongside the barren, gloomy *femme fatale* was the feminized *S*-line, vivifying nineteenth-century culture in a new kind of 'tempestuous loveliness of terror' through what would

Loïe Fuller whirls in her Serpentine Dance, as drawn by W. H. Bradley c. 1895.

become the twentieth-century obsession: movement. The dancer Ida Rubenstein, in the 1920s, appeared on stage wound in mummy bands, which she would sensually unwind with serpent-like movements. This was a take on American Loïe Fuller's turn of the century 'Serpentine Dance', an exceptionally celebrated act, in which she and her dancers would run back and forth across the stage, under changing coloured floodlights, dressed in long, wafting cloth and making the illuminated, diaphanous material rhythmically undulate. As Fuller's body disappeared in her mass of veils, the archaic serpentine principle came alive again: female, serpent and moving process cohered into one indistinguishable whole. This dance was so important that Dulac cited it as *the* precursor to cinema because it was the first art solely determined by manipulation of movement and light. Current film scholars, such as Tom Gunning, defend this idea.[9] So the nineteenth-century serpent-woman

comes full circle with Loïe Fuller and remains the Snake
Goddess in all aspects. As the classic *femme fatale* she is undead,
inhuman, fearsome, deadly, timeless, above retribution, and as
the source of creativity in dance and raw cinema, her *S*-line is
daemonic, regenerative, pro-generative and energized. As both
extremes, this serpent-woman is elementally sexual, as death

and as life. This overt ophidianism diminished in the 1930s. Marlene Dietrich didn't need props to tell the viewer that she was a seducer/slayer. The *femme fatale* of 1940s and '50s *film noir* didn't need animal accoutrements either, but the snake-woman re-emerged in other, gamier movies. She did not escape punishment this time and was either killed or humbled into housewifery. These films went from the subtle, such as Preston Sturge's 1941 sex comedy, *The Lady Eve*, to the obvious, Robert Siodmak's 1944 high camp *Cobra Woman* starring Maria Montez. In *Lady Eve*, Barbara Stanwyck, a confidence trickster, snake-oils her way into the life of timid herpetologist, Henry Fonda, who sums himself up with 'snakes are my life'. Though Fonda is the 'snake-man', Stanwyck sexually controls him as a classic snake *femme fatale*. Her true authority, however, is defined by the male aura of a tight crime operation (Fonda is indeed her 'mouse') until she comes clean. With marriage, her status falls to spouse. *Cobra Woman*, though in a schlock format, has much the same structure where the autonomous woman is demoted while the wife woman is promoted. In it Montez, as the evil Snake Queen of an isolated island, dies while her virtuous twin, about to be married, lives.

No matter what the topic, serpent films commonly uphold folklore tropes of sex, women, health, evil eyes, false unions, bound polarities and curses. Sidney Furie's Z-grade English *The Snake Woman* (1960) or the Mexican *Snake People* (1970) (with Boris Karloff) retained the woman as eerie and superior (combining evil and good) with a Medusan whammy stare. Though played for scares, each carried a medicine subplot (venom as cure for insanity or heart attack). By the 1970s, the snake-in-film was a vehicle for sexploitation, a trait that remains today, in various forms from art house cinema to straight-to-video pap. *Black Cobra* (1976) with Laura Gemser, though strictly soft porn and set in Hong Kong penthouses, replayed classic snake plot points that go back thousands of years: sexual woman, old woman, vengeful snake, parted lovers and retribution. In the film Gemser, a gentle erotic snake dancer (once instructed by a crone mentor), delivers a terrible death by snake, is rejected by her sometime lover and dies. Movies such as Ken Russell's *The Lair of the White Worm* (1988) and Ridley Scott's futuristic *Blade Runner* (1982) also brutally revived the snake *femme fatale*. In *The Lair of the White Worm*, taken from Bram Stoker's *fin-de-siècle* novel, the semi-ophidian Snake Priestess disguises herself as an aristocrat and, in *Blade Runner*, an illegal female android burlesques with a large, artificial snake. Both women die horrific deaths.

Woman and snake as continuing sexual analogue: an erotic dancer transforms into a serpent in Robert Rodriguez's 1996 film *From Dusk till Dawn*.

As the literal snake-woman disappeared as a cinema character, she vaguely re-emerged in two parts – snake and woman – in banal horror. In the 1990s, films like *Anaconda* and *Anaconda II* (starring Jennifer Lopez) sported snake monsters surrounded by sexy women. In 2004, *Anacondas* followed the same formula. They all enjoy the theme of the to-be-defeated snake. Usually a band of urbanites, plus one hardened outbacker, possibly an alcoholic, boat down the Amazon or other jungle river for pleasure or science into a remote area that has been taken over by snakes or by one snake. After much slaughter and some sex, the snake is destroyed. *Anacondas* showed a sign of the times, however, in favouring romance over porn, having the woman rescue the man and bringing a pharmaceutical company into the story. The Chinese *Green Snake* (1993), with Maggie Cheung as a strong snake being transformed into a beautiful woman, relies on many old snake myth components: her character is sexual (like the 1920s *femme fatale*, she tempts men beyond endurance), she heals, she saves her brother-in-law from death by retrieving the desolate plant of life, she controls sea and rain and her character arc is in her unprecedented mingling of evil and good, compassion and indifference. In Robert Rodriguez's *From Dusk till Dawn* (1996), there was a mild return to the old snake-woman when a minor character, a sexy dancer, becomes a snake, but only as a means to instil a weird, unpredictable atmosphere.

The to-be-defeated serpent, with or without women, is always a favourite subject. It can be miniscule or it can be vast. In the film *Sssssss* (1973), the lethal serpent lay within when a scientific madman, doomed to die along with his monstrous creation, turned a man into a cobra. By the new century, this battle transferred comfortably to cyberspace, which, like a parallel cosmos, also has super serpents. In 2004, the

The snake is within in Bernard Kowalski's 1973 horror film *Sssssss*.

Mydoom Worm, a devastating computer virus able to wipe out entire systems with ease swept the Internet. Its medieval name 'Worm' (from Old English *wyrm* and Old High German *würm*, both meaning snake) signifies that though few would know its origins the mythic being is not out of our consciousness. 'Worm' evokes the primordial blindsnake, a giant depicted in films like *Tremors* (1990) and *Dune* (1984), and its name both inspires fear and promises triumph, the process

The primordial blindsnake in David Lynch's 1984 film *Dune*.

implicit in the defeated Lambton Worm, Fafner Würm and Chaos Serpent. The defeatable cosmic snake, still active in the Christian icon of St George killing the dragon-serpent, also lives on in the Mydoom Worm. In some cases, the defeated serpent becomes a not-to-be-defeated serpent. With the uniquely American rattlesnake as an emblem of colonial tenacity, some Revolutionary War regimental flags flashed the words 'Don't Tread on Me' set beneath a ready-to-strike rattle-snake, and the Texas state flag stills displays that image and logo, warning that Texans will strike if disturbed. Benjamin Franklin cartooned an early version of the American patriot snake in the 1751 September issue of his *Pennsylvania Gazette*, which showed a looped snake slashed into eight chunks. Its caption: 'Join, or Die'.

But the truly indefatigable serpent lies in science (where it began) and seems to be thriving in the macro of physics and the micro of biology. 'Worm holes', time-travelling chutes in the

space-time continuum, are conceived as tunnels able to draw an object from one place in time into another place in time. Their designation as 'worm' returns this blend of space and time back to its archaic source where the original 'serpent-worm' cohered both the universe and its invisible processes. This crossing of prosaic boundaries mirrors the Mayan Vision Serpent's penetration of all strata, a concept that in turn mirrors the latest String Theory, which views time as simultaneous, separated only by porous membranes. Jeremy Narby, at the other extreme, argues that the prehistoric super snake is a metaphor for DNA (another coiling, indestructible life force) and that the serpent symbol is simply real science portrayed in mythic terms. He finds basic molecular biology in ophidian mysticism, especially in Australian Aboriginal x-ray drawings, which use what he terms 'biological imagery' such as double helixes and chromosome shapes to inscribe this divine animal. Narby suggests that ecstatic shamanic visions are not hallucinatory but actually apprehend the molecular level and *see* into its 'animate

Rudolf Nureyev in a chic *outré* snakeskin outfit, 1969.

essences' or 'spirits'[10] (as they are called by shamans). These microscopic processes are then rendered as a cosmic snake. Certainly the curled caduceus of Europe and Asia, a Neolithic image, affects a helix structure. Given the evidence over centuries of the snake as primal to the imagination's search for esoteric order, this is not such a wild theory.

But clothing has been the dark horse in carrying old serpent themes. Snakeskin was a rage in the 1920s and again in the 1950s. In the 1960s, its success was due in some part to radical English designer Ossie Clarke who turned society onto the serpent look after finding rolls of snakeskin in a old warehouse in 1967. He used the skin extensively in his jackets, belts and clothes, dressing Twiggy in a python maxi coat trimmed with fox fur in 1969 and pushing 1970s excesses by outfitting Bianca Jagger in a snakeskin jumpsuit in 1973. By the twenty-first century, snake patterns had a fashion resurgence. Snake jewellery was in again. Snakeskin prints or the real thing covered every kind of accessory such as purses, belts, hats and shoes (as diverse as sneakers and t-straps) and were the material for every kind of clothing. Tom Ford's farewell Gucci show featured bejewelled serpent appliquéd gowns and asymmetric patchworks of chiffon, snakeskin, beading and fur, similar in cut to the outfits of the noir *femme fatale* – long, clinging, sleeveless and low cut. These, in turn, echoed early seductress dresses of the 1910s. Costume designer Clare West, in 1912, glamorized the exotic *femme fatale* outfit for actresses like Gloria Swanson, who would slink across a salon in revealing, form-fit gowns cut with dangling, asymmetric sleeves inset with snakeskin, fur and beads.

Menswear too took to the snake. Men's suits in snakeskin prints appeared on the streets in 2003. But a different story, and a different mode, can be traced in this style. Greek superstition holds that snakeskin (especially with eyes intact) will repel the evil eye, mirroring the Medusan double look as both fatal and protective. This idea accompanies today's snakeskin male attire when it flags a renegade hero, sometimes tragic, evidenced in films such as Sidney Lumet's 1959 *Fugitive Kind* based on Tennessee Williams's play, *Orpheus Descending*. His allegory retells the Orpheus myth of his descent into Hell to regain his dead lover. In *Orpheus Descending*, he tries to save a woman married to the town's dying mogul, a man whom the play specifically represents as King of the Underworld. In the film, Marlon Brando, as Val, a travelling misfit, wears a snakeskin jacket to suggest not only his uniqueness but also his chthonic identity as a latter-day consort to the (Snake) Queen of the

Marlon Brando as Val, the snakeskin-wearing consort of Anna Magnani's Queen of the Underworld, in Sidney Lumet's 1959 film *The Fugitive Kind*.

Nicholas Cage in David Lynch's 1990 film *Wild at Heart*, the 1980s version of the snakeskin-wearing misfit hero.

Underworld. In *Escape from New York*, John Carpenter's 1981 futuristic horror fantasy, the travelling misfit, played by Kurt Russell, is called Snake Plissken. A self-sufficient, asocial anti-hero, he also must descend into Hell, this time fashioned as a lawless Manhattan island converted into a giant maximum-security prison where he retrieves a feminized, milk-toast US president, played by Donald Pleasance. In David Lynch's *Wild At Heart* (1990), Nicholas Cage, another travelling misfit, wears a snakeskin jacket and journeys, with his girlfriend, through what some have termed a landscape of Hell.[11] This same misfit-hero appears in the cartoon show *The Simpsons*. The good-looking young thief, named Snake, constantly in and out of jail, is a stock character. He sports Elvis Presley hair, a posh accent, bad boy street clothes of the 1950s (rolled up sleeves, jeans and t-shirt) and a giant arm-length tattoo of an open-mouthed, fanged snake down his right arm. Snake also descends into Hell, i.e. prison, where he often sojourns.

This chthonic snake-hero is an old character, out of early Greece. Harrison reveals how, as patriarchy overtook the Hellenistic world, heroine worship abated and hero worship rose and though heroine's tombs were still places of veneration, new ones were no longer built. With this transition, the hero (who, like snake hero Hercules, was able to straddle life and death) assumed the heroine's qualities as well as a snake form whenever he was 'in' his tomb. The snake hero was a death figure, a normalized role for any larger than life protagonist in that era and a vestige of the Snake Goddess's infernal nature. The twentieth-century snake-heroes have similar attributes. Set up as so misfit that they defy death, they always walk a line between the living and the dead.

As the 'fatal' of the animalized *femme fatale* diminished in the last century, the voluptuous *femme fatale* also vanished, replaced by a compliant adolescent silhouette. In 1982, Richard Avedon photographed superstar Natassia Kinski wrapped in a giant python but her body gave the appearance of a young girl. The March 2004 cover of *Esquire* revived this lacklustre child-woman with a naked Brooke Shields (once child model) draped in a green boa. Thin hipped and weakly pouty, she was everything the serpent femme was not – unthreatening and blandly sexual. The message was unclear. Was this to show men that the serpent-woman was kaput? At the 2003 MTV Awards, this seemed not so. Singer Britney Spears, in a slave girl outfit, hefted a large albino python on her shoulders. Less a bid for Eros, the display acted as an unintended mimic of holy gestures using serpents, such as those used by Mayan priests, perhaps to signify the towering of women in the pop world.

But the snake hero is the one who seems to have taken the place of the dangerous *femme*, albeit in a subdued, wannabee way. Both hero and *femme fatale* are created as outsider figures, between normal and abnormal or living and dead. But the anti-hero only wears the lifeless snakeskin or the snake name, a ritual masqueing, through a costume, to partake in something forbidden to the masquer but nevertheless intensely desired. Conversely, the *femme fatale* wears the living animal itself. They are a unit, one being. The anti-hero visits the underworld. His greatness shows in that he can withstand it. But the *femme fatale* *is* the underworld. She steps from life to death with ease and seems unfazed by the sorrows of alienation.

The symbolic snake won't 'lie quiet' even in its deceptively easy contemporary categories of slander, virility, misogyny, beauty and defeat. Its vast history deepens any image and it is obvious that this history sways the meaning whether apparent or not. The cosmic snake as omniscient female and the serpentine line as eternal *dasein* never recede. They infuse culture and

The snake as power: a Mayan priest or god lifts a huge snake, decoration on a polychromatic pottery vase, 8th century AD, Guatemala.

A piece of New York graffiti celebrates open snake jaws, 2003.

The snake as power: Britney Spears holds a python during a performance.

subvert prejudices in ways that point to an almost inconceivable permanence, declaring that the snake, with its glory and its terror, is dear to us. The serpentine line underlies all the ideas enumerated in this book. As an *S*, a zig zag or a spiral, across millennia, it seems to so excite and so pacify the human mind that, more than anything else, it may account for the attraction to the serpent symbol. Why? The *S*-line is about order, the most beloved cultural precept of all, and furthermore about order as movement, a utopian ideal grasped in the Neolithic, and possibly even the Palaeolithic, and still pursued today. The *S*-line perfectly suited the need to scope the overwhelming cosmos. It encompassed time and space with brevity and accuracy, it was continuous, alinear, vibrant and dimensional. It contained the ultimate structure of all snake symbolism – fusion: fusion of time, of space, of elements, of opposites and of symbiosis. It was (and still is) about transmutation. The serpentine body as a spatial corpus, from its first mythic conception, drew together universal parts, reconciled polarities of life-death, sickness-health, mortality-immortality and acted as a conduit between time lived and time immemorial. Even as it was allegedly destroyed, its body purified the next creation in the sacred combat myths of India, America, Europe, the Middle East, Asia and Africa where, through the snake corpse, new order arose from the old. Its swallowing resurrected the soul. Its edible heart conquered temporality through its gift of second sight. Its flesh turned back the clock and made one young. Its presence activated the cycle of life and death, harmonized chaos, and sparked transfiguration, rejuvenation, realignment and synthesis.

Nothing seems beyond the snake's reach. It cuts through material and mystic layers. As the living snake lives in almost every type of geography, the symbolic snake lives at every metaphysical level. It fills visionary space, cyberspace, quantum space and biological space. As the physicist Kekule realized, over a hundred years ago, the serpent remains the great common denominator, upon which the mind ceaselessly relies. With all the new discoveries, hypotheses and borrowings, and with the taproot of history in every contemporary serpent icon, the super snake of mythic times is far, far from gone.

Here's to the serpentine line. Long may it live!

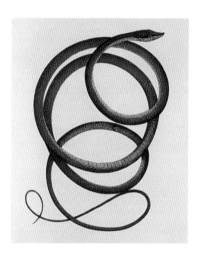

Timeline of the Snake

c. 100 million BC	c. 23 million BC	c.15,000 BC	c.11,000 BC
Snakes appear with lizard characteristics, elongated body, heightened sensory organs, extremely truncated limbs and tiny eyes	Age of Snakes: the contemporary ophidian family tree branches out; advanced, venomous snake develops	Palaeolithic culture carves realistically etched snake on bones; marked, snake-like bones used as probable shamanic lunar calendars. Snake probably used in rituals regarding branch or plants (as life icons) and associated with seasonal change. Multiple zigzags on cave walls	Taï plaque, a potential solar/lunar calendar which reads in a serpentine line, could show beginnings of mythic creation serpent and first graphic abstraction of snake as time animal

c. 900 BC	c. 600 BC	c.458 BC	c. 200 BC	c.100 BC	c. 1000 AD
The book of Genesis depicts snake as satanic force	Gaia's shrine at Delphi, with its sacred Python, is usurped by Apollo	Aeschylus's *Orestea* sanctifies change from matristic to patristic rule through snake imagery	Hannibal engages in biological warfare by throwing venomous snakes in earthen pots at the enemy	Kulkulcan, precursor to Quetzalcoatl, is the incarnate Vision Serpent, the core of Mayan (and Central American) metaphysical philosophy and kingship	Persian *Book of Their'que* shows snake-based remed as potential cure for severe ailment (such as leprosy) and snakebite

1922	1952	1959	1969	1970s	1972
Freud likens Medusa's severed, snaky head to the female vulva and to male castration fears	Jung refers to the unconscious as 'Lamia', an ancient female serpent monster	Sidney Lumet's film, *Fugitive Kind*, begins a genre of sexual, anti-hero males who wear snakeskin	English designer Ossie Clarke popularizes snakeskin, dressing Twiggy in a floor-length python-skin coat	Venom's enzymes begin to be explored in medical treatments for illness as diverse as Alzheimer's, stroke and cancer	Worldwic ban on snakeskir traffic

c. 3100 BC	c. 3000 BC	c. 2000 BC	c. 1500 BC
First written myths establish snake as the supreme cosmic force. Sumerian *Enuma elish* describes creation as primal water activated by female serpent Tiamat. Egyptian creation myth similar 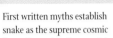	Mythical Chinese serpent-tailed royals, Fu-Xi and Niu-kua, commence civilization and introduce governing social principles, especially matrimony	The Hindu *Vedas*, Supreme Being Vishnu, 'lies in lap of the serpent' Images/tales of serpent and Tree of life or Elixir/ Plant of Life abound	Advanced Minoan civilization has snake handler/ Snake Goddess religion Moses carries bronze serpent on pole during the Israelite exodus

1500s	1753	1837	1890s	1913
The Italian Mannerists, especially Michelangelo, hail the *figura serpentinata* as the supreme artistic line, building a new philosophy around it. This influences centuries of art and underlies elements of contemporary painting and writing	William Hogarth extols the *S*-line as the quintessence of aesthetics in *The Analysis of Beauty*	Italian scientist Felix Fontana writes his *Treatise on Viper Venom*, which for the first time recognizes that venom congeals blood	European painters depict *femmes fatales* as naked, semi-supernatural women draped in snakes. The snake loses its Romantic ambiguity and is an analogue for female sexuality as daemonic	French film serial *Fântomas* features the Phantom, a master criminal who employs a pet boa, the Silent Executioner, to kill

1982	1990s	1999	2002	2003	2004
Richard Avedon photographs Natassia Kinski wrapped in a giant python. The poster is a huge hit	Monster snake films such as *Tremors* and *Anaconda I* and *II* are popular	Vietnam and China (temporarily) ban the lucrative snake export trade as the popularity of snake cuisine is decimating the species	US army invades Afghanistan in search of Osama bin Laden under the rubric 'Operation Anaconda'	Vietnam and China lift snake export ban At the MTV Awards, singer Britney Spears carries a large albino python	Mydoom Worm, a devastating computer virus, sweeps the Internet Snake handling religions continue in America, India and Southeast Asia

References

INTRODUCTION

1 Quoted in Findlay Russell, *Snake Venom Poisoning* (Great Neck, NY, 1983) p. 527.
2 *Ibid.*, p.1.

2 MYTHIC SNAKE

1 Erich Neuman, *The Great Mother* (Princeton, NJ, 1963), p. 41.
2 Alexander Marshack, *The Roots of Civilization* (New York, 1972), p. 224.
3 As discussed in Richard Rudgley, *The Lost Civilizations of the Stone Age* (New York, 1999), p. 103–4.
4 Marija Gimbutus, *The Civilization of the Goddess* (San Francisco, 1991), p. 249.
5 Neuman *The Great Mother*, p. 145.
6 Jane Ellen Harrison, *Themis (*London, 1963), p. 429.
7 From *Vishnu Purana 1.2 [64–65]*, quoted in Alain Danielou, *Hindu Polytheism* (Princeton, NJ, 1964), p.163.
8 *Ibid.*, p.163.
9 E. A. Wallis Budge, *Gods of Egypt* (New York, 1988), I, p. 440.
10 Marija Gimbutus. *The Language of the Goddess* (New York, 1989).
11 From the *Devi Bhagavata Purana 1.1 [179]*, quoted in Danielou, *Hindu Polytheism*, p. 255.

12 Walter Burkett, *The Mystery Religions* (Cambridge, 1987), p. 106.

13 Harrison, *Themis*, p. 432.

14 Wallis Budge, *Gods of Egypt*, I, p. 257.

15 Quoted in Merlin Stone, *When God Was a Woman* (New York, 1976).

16 Harrison, *Themis*, p. 381.

17 Carl Jung, *Symbols of Transformation*, trans. R.F.F. Hull (Princeton, NJ, 1978), p. 298.

18 Harrison, *Themis*, p. 311.

19 Monica Sjöö, *The Great Cosmic Mother* (San Francisco, 1987), p. 144.

20 Harrison, *Themis*, p. 381.

21 Hans Zimmer, *Myths and Symbols in Indian Art and Civilization* (Princeton, NJ, 1946), p. 67.

22 Jane Ellen Harrison, *Prolegomena to the Study of Greek Religion* (Princeton, NJ, 1991), p. 18. Zeus Melichius (the Gentle One) was the converse of Zeus Maimactes (the Enraged), and was his underworld aspect, worshipped at Corinth as a gigantic serpent. It was Zeus Melichius who coupled with Semele (daughter of Demeter) to produce the god Dionysius.

23 *Ibid.*, p. 233.

24 Aeschylus, *Oresteia,* trans. Richmond Lattimore (Chicago, 1970), pp. 136–9.

25 Harrison, *Prolegomena*, p. 236.

26 Linda Schele and David Freidel, A *Forest of Kings: The Untold Story of the Ancient Maya* (New York, 1990), p. 68.

27 *Ibid.*, p. 395.

28 Aaron was Moses' spokesman and carried a rod that turned into a snake.

29 Barbara Elkins, quoted in Fred Brown and Jeanne McDonald, *The Serpent Handlers: Three Families and their Faith* (Winston-Salem, NC, 2000), p. 251.

30 *Ibid.*, p. 251.

3 VENOMOUS SNAKE

1 André Ménez, *The Subtle Beast: Snake, from Myth to Medicine* (London, 2003), p. 91.
2 Jane Ellen Harrison, *Themis* (London, 1963), p. 24. She is quoting Lucian.
3 Ménez, *The Subtle Beast*, p. 91.
4 From Marie Phisalix, *The Vipers of France* (Paris, 1940), quoted in Chen-Yuan Lee (ed.), *Snake Venoms* (Berlin, 1979), p. 5.
5 Daniel Defoe, *A Journal of the Plague Year* [1722] (London, 1970), p. 248.

4 EDIBLE SNAKE

1 Paraphrased from 'The Dragon, the Tiger and the Phoenix', Hong Kong Tourist Association (2001).
http://www.familytravelforum.com/hknewyeardining.html

5 PET SNAKE

1 Care information thanks to Snakebabe.com

6 VOGUE SNAKE

1 Quoted by Richard Benjamin, *Art Bulletin*, LXXV/2 (June 1993).
2 Translation by Simon Burt.
3 William Shakespeare, *Julius Caesar*, II.i.
4 Jean Chevalier and Alain Gheerbrant, *The Penguin Dictionary of Symbols*, trans. John Buchanan-Brown (London, 1969), p. 845.
5 Erich Neuman, *The Great Mother* (Princeton, NJ, 1963), p. 39.
6 Lucy Hughes-Hallett, *Cleopatra Histories, Dreams and Distortions* (London, 1990), p. 131.
7 Bram Dijkstra, *Idols of Perversity: Fantasies of Feminine Evil in Fin-de-Siècle Culture* (Oxford, 1986), p. 304.

8 George MacDonald, *Phantastes and Lilith* (Grand Rapids, MI, 1964), pp. 372–3.

9 Tom Gunning, 'Light, Motion, Cinema!: The Heritage of Loïe Fuller and Germaine Dulac', *Framework*, XLVI /1 (Spring 2005).

10 Jeremy Narby, *The Cosmic Serpent: DNA and the Origins of Knowledge* (New York, 1998), p. 117.

11 Leonard Maltin, *1999 Movie and Video Guide* (New York, 1999), p. 1528.

Bibliography

Aeschylus, *Oresteia*, trans. Richmond Lattimore (Chicago, 1970)

Alban, Gillian, *Melusine the Serpent Goddess in A. S. Byatt's 'Possession' and in Mythology* (Lanham, MD, 2003)

Alexiou, Stylianos, *Minoan Civilization*, trans. Cressida Ridley (Heraklion, 1978)

Apulieus, *The Golden Ass*, trans. Robert Graves (Harmondsworth, 1951)

Arnheim, Rudolf, *Visual Thinking* (Berkeley, CA, 1969)

Baring-Gould, Sabine, *Curious Myths of the Middle Ages* (New York, 1976)

Benjamin, Roger, *Art Bulletin*, LXXV/2 (June 1993)

Benton, Michael, *The Penguin Historical Atlas of the Dinosaurs* (London, 1996)

Brown, Fred and Jeanne McDonald, *The Serpent Handlers: Three Families and their Faith* (Winston-Salem, NC, 2000)

Buchler, Ira R. and Kenneth Madock, *The Rainbow Serpent A Chromatic Piece* (The Hague, 1978)

Budge, E. A. Wallis, *Babylonian Story of the Deluge and the Epic of Gilgamesh with an Account of the Royal Libraries of Nineveh* (London, 1929)

——, *The Egyptian Book of the Dead* (New York, 1967)

——, *From Fetish to God in Ancient Egypt* (New York, 1988)

——, *The Gods of the Egyptians*, 2 vols (New York, 1969)

——, *Osiris and the Egyptian Resurrection*, 2 vols (New York, 1973)

Burkert, Walter, *Ancient Mystery Cults* (Cambridge, 1987)

Campbell, Joseph, *Masks of God: Occidental Mythology* (London, 1965)

Cavendish, Richard, *The Magical Arts: Western Occultism and the Occultists* (London, 1967)

Chevalier, Jean and Alain Gheerbrant, *The Penguin Dictionary of Symbols*, trans. John Buchanan-Brown (London, 1969)

Cirlot, J. E., *A Dictionary of Symbols* (London, 1990)

Coe, Michael D., *The Maya* (London, 1973)

Coe, Ralph T., *Scared Circles*, Arts Council of Great Britain exh. cat., Hayward Gallery, London, October 1976–January 1977

Cooper, J. C., *An Illustrated Encyclopedia of Traditional Symbols* (London, 1997)

Courlander, Harold, *A Treasury of Afro-American Folklore* (New York, 1996)

Covington, Dennis, *Salvation on Sand Mountain: Snake Handling and Redemption in Southern Appalachia* (New York, 1995)

Crawford, Ogs, *The Eye Goddess* (London, 1957)

Cumont, Franz, *The Mysteries of Mithra*, trans. Thomas J. McCormack (New York, 1956)

Daniélou, Alain, *Hindu Polytheism* (Princeton, NJ, 1964)

D'Alviella, Count Goblet, *The Migration of Symbols* (New York, 1956)

Defoe, Daniel, *A Journal of the Plague Year* [1722] (London, 1970)

De Rola, Stanislas Klossowski, *Alchemy: The Secret Art* (London, 1973)

de Santillana, Giorgio and Herth von Dechend, *Hamlet's Mill: An Essay on Myth and the Frame of Time* (London, 1969)

——, *The Origins of Scientific Thought From Anaximander to Proclus, 600 BC to AD 500* (New York, 1961)

Dickinson, Emily, *The Complete Poems* (London, 1982)

Diop, Cheikh Anta, *Civilization or Barbarism: An Authentic Anthropology*, trans. Yaa-Lengi Meema Ngemi (New York, 1991)

Dijkstra, Bram, *Idols of Perversity: Fantasies of Feminine Evil in Fin-de Siècle Culture* (Oxford, 1986)

——, *Evil Sisters: The Threat of Female Sexuality in Twentieth Century Culture* (New York, 1996)

Eliot, T. S., *The Wasteland and Other Poems* (London, 1972)

Elliot, T. J., trans., *A Medieval Bestiary* (Boston, 1971)

Ellis Davidson, H. R., *Gods and Myths of Northern Europe*
(Harmondsworth, 1979)

Erdoes, Richard and Alfonso Ortiz, *American Indian Myths and
Legends* (New York, 1984)

Ernst, Carl H. and George R. Zug, *Snakes in Question* (Washington,
DC, 1996)

Euripides, *Electra, The Phoenician Women, The Bacchae*, ed. Richmond
Lattimore (Chicago, 1970)

Evans, Ivor H., *Brewer's Dictionary of Phrase and Fable* (London, 1981)

Fontenrose, Joseph, *Python: A Study of Delphic Myth and Its Origins*
(Berkeley, CA, 1959)

Fox, Robin Lane, *Pagans and Christians* (New York, 1987)

Frankfort, Henri, *Before Philosophy* (London, 1964)

Frazer, James George, *The New Golden Bough*, abridged (New York, 1964)

Freud, Sigmund, 'Medusa's Head', in *Collected Papers*, vol. XI (New
York, 1959)

Getty, Adele, *Goddess Mother of Living Nature* (London, 1990)

Gimbutus, Marija, *Gods and Goddesses of Old Europe 6500–3500 BC:
Myths and Cult Images* (London, 1982)

——, *The Civilization of the Goddess: The World of Old Europe* (San
Francisco, 1991)

——, *The Language of the Goddess* (London, 1989)

Graves, Robert, *The Greek Myths*, 2 vols (London, 1955)

——, *The White Goddess* (London, 1957)

Greene, Harry W., *Snakes: The Evolution of Mystery in Nature*
(Berkeley, CA, 1997)

Hall, James, *Hall's Dictionary of Subjects and Symbols in Art* (London,
1991)

Harrison, Jane Ellen, *Prolegomena to the Study of Greek Religion*
(Princeton, NJ, 1991)

——, *Themis* (London, 1963)

Higgins, Reynold, *Minoan and Mycenaean Art* (London, 1989)

Hoang Ha Linh, 'Snakes in Life' http://www.nhandan.org.vn

Hooke, S. H., *Middle Eastern Mythology* (Harmondsworth, 1966)

Honour, Hugh, *Romanticism* (London, 1981)

Hughes-Hallett, Lucy, *Cleopatra Histories, Dreams and Distortions* (London, 1990)

Hunt, Lynn, ed., *The Invention of Pornography: Obscenity and the Origins of Modernity, 1500–1800* (New York, 1993)

Johnson, Buffie, *Lady of the Beasts: Ancient Images of the Goddess and her Sacred Animals* (San Francisco, 1981)

Jung, C. G., *Psychology and Alchemy*, trans R.F.C. Hull (London, 1953)

——, *Symbols of Transformation*, trans. R.F.C. Hull (Princeton, NJ, 1990)

Kerényi, Karl, 'The Trickster in Relation to Greek Mythology', in *The Trickster: A Study in American Indian Mythology* (New York, 1972)

Keesey, Pam, *Vamps: An Illustrated History of the Femme Fatale* (San Francisco, 1997)

Kirk, G. S., *Myth: Its Meaning and Function in Ancient and Other Cultures* (Cambridge, 1970)

Kluckhohn, Clyde and Dorothea Leighton, *The Navaho* (New York, 1962)

Klum, Mattias, 'King Cobras, Feared, Revered', *National Geographic* (November 2001)

Kramer, Samuel Noah, ed., *Mythologies of the Ancient World* (New York, 1961)

Lee, Chen-Yuan, ed. *Snake Venoms* (Berlin, 1979)

Lerner, Gerda, *The Creation of Patriarchy* (New York, 1986)

Lessing, G. E., *Laokoön, oder über die Grenzen der Malerie und Poesie* (Munich, 1766)

Lopez-Pedraza, *Hermes and His Children* (Zurich, 1977)

Mackenzie, Donald A., *China and Japan Myths and Legends* (London, 1923)

MacDonald, Mark, 'Year of the Snake Hits Home in Town of Viper Eateries',
http://www.undp.org.vn/mlist/envirovlc/012001/post76.htm

MacDonald, George, *Phantastes and Lilith* [1858] (Grand Rapids, MI, 1964)

Marshack, Alexander, *The Roots of Civilization: The Cognitive Beginnings of Man's First Art: Symbol and Notation* (New York, 1972)

Maspero, Gaston, *Popular Stories of Ancient Egypt*, trans. A. S. Johns
    (New Hyde Park, 1967)

McName, Gregory, ed., *The Serpent's Tale: Snakes in Folklore and
    Literature* (Athens, GA, 2000)

Maltin, Leonard, *Leonard Maltin's 1999 Movie and Video Guide*
    (New York, 1999)

Martin, Elizabeth and Robert Hine, eds, *Oxford Dictionary of Biology*
    (Oxford, 2000)

Mayer, Martin, *Madison Avenue USA* (London, 1961)

Menez, Andre, *The Subtle Beast: Snake, from Myth to Medicine*
    (London, 2003)

Milner, John, *Symbolists and Decadents* (London, 1971)

Minton, Sherman and Madge Minton, *Venomous Reptiles* (New York,
    1969)

Muller, Max and James George Scott, *The Mythology of All Races
    Egyptian and Indo-Chinese*, vol. XII (New York, 1964)

Mundku, Balaji, *The Cult of the Serpent: An Interdisciplinary Survey of
    its Manifestations and Origins* (Albany, NY, 1983)

Murray, Margaret, *The Splendour That Was Egypt* (London, 1973)

Narby, Jeremy, *The Cosmic Serpent: DNA and the Origins of Knowledge*
    (New York, 1998)

Neuman, Erich, *The Great Mother: An Analysis of the Archetype*, trans.
    Ralph Manheim (Princeton, NJ, 1963)

Newman, Paul, *The Hill of the Dragon: An Enquiry* (New York, 1979)

Northcutt, Wendy, *The Darwin Awards: Evolution in Action* (New York,
    2000)

Ovid, *Metamorphoses*, trans. Mary M. Innes (London, 1955)

Owomoyela, Oyekan, *Yoruba Trickster Tales* (Lincoln, NE, 1997)

Pachter, Henry M., *Magic into Science: The Story of Paracelsus* (New
    York, 1951)

Pagels, Elaine, *Adam, Eve, and the Serpent* (London, 1988)

——, *The Gnostic Gospels* (New York, 1989)

Parrinder, Geoffrey, *African Mythology* (London, 1967)

Pausanias, *Guide to Greece*, 2 vols, trans. Peter Levi (London, 1971)

Pearsall, Ronald, *The Worm in the Bud* (London, 1993)

Purce, Jill, *The Mystic Spiral* (London, 1974)

Radin, Paul, *The Trickster: A Study in American Indian Mythology* (New York, 1972)

Reichard, Gladys A., *Navaho Religion: A Study of Symbolism* (New York, 1950)

Rudgley, Richard, *The Lost Civilizations of the Stone Age* (New York, 1999)

Rundle Clarke, R. T., *Myth and Symbol in Ancient Egypt* (London, 1978)

Russell, Findlay, *Snake Venom Poisoning* (Great Neck, NY, 1983)

Schele, Linda and David Freidel, A *Forest of Kings: The Untold Story of the Ancient Maya* (New York, 1990)

Schele, Linda and Mary Ellen Miller, *The Blood of Kings: Dynasty and Ritual in Maya Art* (London, 1992)

Shuttle, Penelope and Peter Redgrove, *The Wise Wound: Menstruation and Everywoman* (London, 1978)

Singer, June, *Androgyny: Toward a New Theory of Sexuality* (Garden City, NJ, 1977)

Sjöö, Monica and Barbara Mor, *The Great Cosmic Mother* (San Francisco, 1987)

Smith, Morton, *The Secret Gospel* (Wellingborough, 1985)

——, *Jesus the Magician* (Wellingborough, 1985)

Snook, John, *African Snake Stories* (New York, 1971)

Stone, Merlin, *When God Was a Woman* (New York, 1976)

Stancioff, Marion, 'The Marion Stancioff Symbol Archives', Warburg Institute, London

Strafford, Peter, *Snakes* (London, 2000)

Tansley, David V., *Subtle Body Essence and Shadow* (London, 1984)

Thorpe, R. S., W. Wüster and A. Malhotra, eds, *Venomous Snakes: Ecology, Evolution and Snakebite* (Oxford, 1997)

Topsell, Edward, *The Historie of Serpents* (London, 1608)

Twitchell, James B., *Adcult USA: The Triumph of American Advertising in American Culture* (New York, 1996)

Tyndale, William, *Tyndale's New Testament* [1534] (New Haven, CT, 1991)

Vaillant, G. C., *The Aztecs of Mexico* (Harmondsworth, 1951)

Walker, Barbara G., *The Woman's Encyclopedia of Myths and Secrets* (San Francisco, 1983)

——, *The Crone Woman of Age, Wisdom, and Power* (San Francisco, 1985)

Wand, J.W.C., *A History of the Early Church to AD 500* (London, 1982)

Waters, Frank, *Masked Gods: Navaho and Pueblo Ceremonialism* (New York, 1975)

Weigle, Marta, *Spiders and Spinsters: Women and Myth* (Albuquerque, NM, 1982)

Wolkstein, Diane and Samuel Kramer, *Inanna: Queen of Heaven and Earth* (London, 1982)

Yates, Frances, *Rosicrucian Enlightenment* (St Albans, 1975)

——, *Giordano Bruno and the Hermetic Tradition* (London, 1964)

Zimmer, Hans, *Myths and Symbols in Indian Art and Civilization* (Princeton, NJ, 1946)

Zug, George R. and Carl Ernest, *Snakes in Question* (Washington, DC, 1996)

Recipes and Cocktails

RECIPES

The embargo against eating snake in the West is so strong that recipes in English were unavailable, even in the most exhaustive international cookbooks. The recipes below could only be obtained through the Internet.

JAPAN

This 400-year-old recipe from Japan uses the highly venomous red habu.

Habu and Sake[1]
Raw, high-energy mountain potato, grated into a gel, mixed with raw quail egg and smelt fish eggs. One glass of sake fermented with the poison of the habu snake from Okinawa is drunk to finish this small meal.

NEW GUINEA

Paua Sup (Power Soup)[2]
Tie a python to a pole, skin the animal alive and remove excess fat. Keep gall bladder aside for medicinal purposes.
Chop snake into one-inch pieces and place in cold water and bring to boil.

Simmer for 3–4 hours. After, discard the water.

Boil head separately and keep the liquid, which is useful against choking.

Meanwhile, prepare another stock from an old chicken, and/or pork scraps, onion, chili, salt and pepper. Skim the fat off this while it is cooking and discard. Cook for 3–4 hours, cool and drain.

Prepare an herb soup of abika cabbage and a large quantity of ginger. Combine all ingredients and reheat.

Brandy may be added.

CHINA

Both the following recipes are from Lee Keung, chef at Hong Kong's famous Summer Palace Restaurant.

Snake Soup[3]
1 oz of each:
Cooked snake meat
Dried fungus
Fish maw
Shredded chicken
Dried mandarin peel
Bamboo shoots
Combine all with 5 oz of boiled snake broth

Deep Fried Snake Meat Balls
5 oz minced prawns
2 oz cooked snake meat
Combine with Chinese brown mushrooms, stir-fry and serve

USA

Furnance Creek Inn's Rattlesnake Empañada[4]
1 pound boneless rattlesnake meat
3 oz raw chicken meat or chicken fat, used as a binder

$^1/_2$ cup each red, yellow and green bell peppers, chopped fine
$^1/_2$ cup nopalitos (cactus), julienned
1 tablespoon ground cumin
1 teaspoon salt
1 teaspoon pepper
1 teaspoon granulated garlic
1 teaspoon chile powder
$^1/_4$ cup lime juice
2 boxes of puff pastry sheets (found in the frozen food section)
$^1/_2$ cup shredded Colby cheese
egg wash (well-beaten eggs)

Preheat oven to 350 degrees.
Grind rattlesnake and chicken together (should look like ground pork when through).
In a skillet, sauté peppers, cactus and meat together about 15 minutes. Add remaining ingredients (minus the pastry and cheese). Cook for 15 to 20 minutes more, drain and let cool.
Add cheese to well drained mixture.
Spread out pastry sheet and cut into 4-inch circles with a biscuit or tart cutter (a tuna can also makes a great cutter).
Brush with egg wash and place some of the mixture in the middle of the pastry circle. Fold over and crimp edges closed.
Bake for about 12 minutes.

GUAM

Fried Snake[5]
1lb skinned snake, cut into 1 inch pieces
1 cup sherry
$^1/_2$ teaspoon Black pepper
$^1/_2$ teaspoon season-all
$^1/_4$ cup lemon juice
$^1/_2$ cup of Italian salad dressing
flour

Marinate pieces of snake in the mixture of sherry, pepper, season-all, lemon juice and Italian dressing for 2 hours.
Drain and dredge with flour.
Fry pieces for about 15 minutes, turning often until brown.
Drain and serve hot.

Snake Adobo
1lb skinned snake, cut into 1 inch pieces
1 tablespoon vinegar or lemon juice
$\frac{1}{2}$ teaspoon of sugar
$\frac{1}{2}$ cup soy sauce
$\frac{1}{4}$ teaspoon black pepper or to taste
2 cloves minced garlic

Boil snake pieces for 30 minutes.
Drain and brown in pan.
Add mixture of vinegar, sugar, garlic, soy sauce and pepper.
Cook for 30 minutes. Serve hot.

COCKTAILS

VIETNAM
Live cobra heart
Shot of vodka
Cobra blood
Mix, drink immediately

JAPAN

Habu Sake
Coil Habu (can be up to 6 feet) in Sake jar
Ferment Habu in sake

Snakebite
4 $\frac{1}{2}$ oz Jack Daniels
1 $\frac{1}{2}$ oz Cointreau
1 $\frac{1}{2}$ oz lime cordial
Shake, strain into tall glass

References

1 Courtesy of Nick Paine, self-described as the 'world's only culinary anthropologist'. http://www.exotickitchen.com/recipes/recipes4.htm
2 Courtesy of Lesley Martin; part of a recipe contest held by the Anahita Gallery in New Mexico.
http://www.anahitagallery.com/ahrecipe04.html
3 Courtesy of the Hong Kong Tourist Association
http://www.familytravelforum.com/hknewyeardining.html
4 Courtesy of Michelle 'Mike' Hanson, chef at Furnace Creek Inn in Death Valley, California.
5 Courtesy of Guan Division of Aquatic and Wildlife Resources.
http://www.mesc.usgs.gov/resources/education/bts/resources/resources.asp

Associations

AMERICAN FEDERATION OF HERPETOCULTURISTS
A nonprofit organization, the AFH represents breeders and keepers of amphibians and reptiles.

AMERICAN SOCIETY OF ICHTHYOLOGISTS AND HERPETOLOGISTS
Oldest international organization for the scientific study of fishes, amphibians and reptiles. Established in 1913.

AUSTRALIAN SOCIETY OF HERPETOLOGISTS
A professional body of practicing herpetologists that promotes the study of amphibians and reptiles.

BRITISH HERPETOLOGICAL SOCIETY
Great Britain's oldest and largest herpetological society, founded in 1947.

SOCIETY FOR THE STUDY OF AMPHIBIANS AND REPTILES (SSAR)
Largest international herpetological society. Established in the USA in 1958 to advance research, conservation and education for amphibians and reptiles. Has the most diverse international programme of publications and activities.

THE HERPETOLOGISTS' LEAGUE
Oldest international organization devoted to studying the biology of amphibians and reptiles. Established in 1936 in the USA.

Websites

http://www.kingsnake.com" www.kingsnake.com
> This is the king of snake sites. It has hundreds of snake links covering everything from breeders to events to current books.

http://www.herpsofnc.org/" http://www.herpsofnc.org/
> This poses and answers questions and facts about snakes. It has many specifics about South Carolina snakes.

http://www.ophiservices.com" www.ophiservices.com
> You can find anything here from snake pet names to herpetological societies to breeding tips and pictures.

http://w.ww.gatormall.com" http://w.ww.gatormall.com
> This site sells snake products.

http://w.ww.exoticmall.com" http://w.ww.exoticmall.com
> This sells snake products, such as accessories, stuffed animals etc.

http://dir.yahoo,com/Science/Biology/Zoology/
> http://dir.yahoo,com/Science/Biology/Zoology/
> Go to Reptiles and Snakes for a variety of information.

Acknowledgements

Thanks to Leslie Dick, Diane Lewis, Jerry Leen, Brian Price, Terrel Seltzer, Marion Stancioff and Angela Della Vacche for their comments and support.

Photo Acknowledgements

The author and publishers wish to express their thanks to the below sources of illustrative material and/or permission to reproduce it. (Some sources uncredited in the captions for reasons of brevity are also given below.)

Photos AP Photo: p. 157 (photo Joe Imel), 182 (photo Beth A. Keiser); photos courtesy of the author: pp. 98, 168 top; drawings by the author: pp. 38 (after Alexander Marshack), 49 (after Linda Williams); Bibliotheque Nationale, Paris, France (Archives Charmet, Ms. Arabe 2964, fol. 17): p. 113; photo Bridgeman Art Library (BAL 163332): p. 113; Musée de Clermont-Ferrand: p. 160; Archaeological Museum, Heraklion: p. 51; photos Library of Congress, Washington, DC: pp. 8 (National Photo Company Collection, LC-USZ62-107746), 46 (Prints and Photographs Division, LC-USZC4-10077), 47 (Work Projects Administration Poster Collection, LC-USZC2-1109), 63 (Prints and Photographs Division, LC-USZ62-90673), 65 (Rare Book and Special Collections Division, LC-USZC4-5347), 72 (Prints and Photographs Division, Edward S. Curtis Collection, LC-USZ 62-52205), 81 (Prints and Photographs Division, LC-USZ 62-106980), 85 (Frank and Frances Carpenter Collection, LC-USZ 62-34388), 86 top (Farm Security Administration – Office of War Information Photograph Collection LC-USF 33-011769-M1), 91 top (photo Hartwell & Hamaker, LC-USZ 62-101334), 102 (Prints and Photographs Division, LC-USZC 2-4043), 112 (Prints and Photographs Division, LC-USZ 62-95184), 155 top (Prints and Photographs Division, Caroline and Erwin Swann Collection of Caricature & Cartoon, LC-USZ

62-85471), (Prints and Photographs Division, Yanker Poster Collection, Gift of Gary Yanker, LC-USZ 62-96338), 177 (LC-USZC 4-5315); Archaeological Museum, Mexico City: p. 60; courtesy of Photofest: 149 top (photo © MCMLXV Walt Disney Productions. World Rights Reserved), 176, 180; photos Rex Features: pp. 6 (Chris Martin Bahr, 377436S), 21 (Sipa Press, 377388A), 28 foot (Keystone/Rex Features, 446268U), 32 (Paul Raffaele, 460613S), 79 (The Travel Library, 426418A), 86 foot (Sipa Press, 173776E), 87 (Sipa Press, 445287B), 107 (Peter Woolrich, 197543A), 117 Sipa Press, 176503B), 125 top (David M. Hayes, 121414R), 125 middle (Richard Jones, 412174J), 125 foot (David M. Hayes, 121414N), 128 (PNS/Rex Features, 447262E), 129 (Charles Sykes, 404326M), 132 (INS News Group Ltd, 296947D), 134 (Sipa Press, 378244B), 135 (Rex Features, 176573A), 149 foot (Granada/Rex Features, 442379B), 165 foot (Patrick Rideaux, 395735C), 178 (Keystone, 438541K); photo © Universal Pictures: p. 174; photo courtesy US National Archives, Washington, DC (Solid Fuels Administration for War, Russell Lee Collection): p. 91 (foot); photos Roger Viollet/Rex Features: pp. 9 (© Bruni/Alinari/Roger-Viollet, 17151-18), 61 (© Collection Roger-Viollet, RBV-07849), 83 (© Collection Roger-Viollet, 4360-14), 88 (© Collection Roger-Viollet, 604-4), 160 (© Collection Roger-Viollet, RBV-01095); photos © Zoological Society of London: pp. 16, 22 (from Krefft, *The snakes of Australia*, Sydney, 1869), 24, 28 top, 30 top left (from Fitzinger, *Bilder-Atlas zur wissenschaftlich-populären Naturgeschichte der Amphibien...* (Vienna, 1864), 30 top right (from Holbrook, *North American Herpetology,* Philadephia, 1842), 30 foot (from Catesby, *Natural History of Carolina, Florida and the Bahama Islands* (London, 1754), 31 (from Owen, *Anatomy of Vertebrates*, vol. 1 (London, 1866), 71, 75 (both from Marco Aurelio Severino, *Vipera pythia . . .* , Padua, 1651), 95 (both from Russell, *An Account of Indian serpents* (London, 1796), 99 (from Catesby, *Natural History of Carolina . . .*), 186 (from Jean de Spix, *Sepentum Brasiliensium species novae . . .* (Munich, 1824).

Index